May you walk in
the green light of the Gospel
Eph. 6:10-18
Audrey Hebbert

This book is so good that it makes me want to go on a mission trip to China so I can climb the Great Wall and eat snake brain! I would also like to be more like Monica, who always puts other people first.

Sydney Schwager, age 12

I thought *Green Light Red Light* was awesome, especially Monica; she's cool! It would be very hard for me to eat puppies or snake brains, though—totally gross!"

Shane Madden, age 14

A very well written book, it puts a clear image in the reader's mind on exactly what China's conditions were at the time, especially the food market. The book makes me miss the crowded streets and cheap haircuts.

Beth Cao, age 15
Native of China

Audrey's debut novel is an effortless read about 16-year-old Erika's first steps on her missions journey. This delight-filled tale serves as a terrific "how-to" book for youths thinking of joining a missions team.

Lucy Lewis, Librarian
Omaha Public Library

I am honored to know the real Monica Moore and thankful she gave permission for this book to be written.

Germaine Saucier, Senior Citizen

Audrey Hebbert chronicles the true-life story of the most unlikely of heroes, a little lady from the Midwest who, standing on the shoulders of such giants of the faith as Hudson Taylor and Gladys Aylward, continues the remarkable story of God's love and redemption in China. *Green Light Red Light* is a true inspiration!

Dave Collins, Pastoral Care Pastor

I believe that there are few things more significant in shaping a teenager into a genuine follower of Jesus than asking them to follow Him in a culture that is radically different than their own. In *Green Light Red Light*, Hebbert gives real insight into the struggles of a teenage girl from the United States being thrown into a foreign culture. This book is an incredible testimony of God's pattern of working in us as he pours us out for others. I would recommend this book for any teenager who is considering a short term missions experience.

Mike Ballard, Senior High Pastor

Through young Erika's time in China we see two cultures connect in their desire for something more besides simply living. This story was a learning experience for me and just plain fun to read.

Dan Gruber, Kids' Pastor

Green Light Red Light is a delightful book. It is a rare combination of exploits of daring evangelism set in a context that is very human and often—in a sanctified sense—very funny. It is the story of God using ordinary people to do extraordinary things in a land where the persecution of believers is a daily reality. Over the years Monica Moore has shared many of her experiences with me personally and the book faithfully reflects her extraordinary ministry. As a grandmother she both challenges the older believer to greater exploits for Christ, and equally challenges the younger generation—who just love her—to invest their lives for the kingdom. This book is a book you will not be able to put down.

Ray Mayhew, Pastor of Biblical Studies

After reading the book, I realize that forgiveness is not easy to learn, but everlasting love from God helps us to forgive and leads us to believe like Monica: an example of God's love.

Mrs. Lu, Hsin-Jung, and Shing-Jye Chen, Ph. D.,
UNO Asst. Professor

Green Light
Red Light

Green Light
Red Light

A STORY OF ADVENTURE AMONG THE STUDENTS OF CHINA

AUDREY HEBBERT

TRESTLE PRESS
LINCOLN, NEBRASKA USA

Green Light Red Light

A Story Of Adventure Among The Students of China

By: Audrey Hebbert

Library of Congress Control Number: 2007906713

Publisher's Cataloging-in-Publication
(Provided by Quality Books, Inc.)

Hebbert, Audrey.
Green light red light : a story of adventure among the students of China / Audrey Hebbert.
p. cm.
SUMMARY: This fictionalized biography tells the story of Monica Moore, an elderly woman who travels to China every summer to serve as a Christian missionary.
LCCN 2007906713
ISBN-13: 978-0-9765222-3-2
ISBN-10: 0-9765222-3-3

1. Women missionaries--China--Juvenile fiction. 2. Older people in missionary work--China--Juvenile fiction. 3. China--Missions--Juvenile fiction. 4. Biographical fiction. [1. Women missionaries--Fiction. 2. Older people in missionary work--Fiction. 3. Missionaries--Fiction. 4. China--Fiction.] I. Title.

PZ7.H3528Gre 2007 [Fic]
QBI07-600252

Printed in the United States of America

Cover Design by: **Nate Perry**

Trestle Press
Lincoln, Nebraska USA

Contents

Dedication

To King Jesus. Without His great work there would be no *Green Light Red Light*.

To the many friends and family of all ages who worked on this project as if it were their own. I won't name you because I might forget someone, but thank you to all. You are a prized part of my friendship circle, and your labor of love will never be forgotten.

Special thanks to Monica Moore (not her real name) who spent hours speaking into a tape recorder, sharing her true-to-life stories about her work around the world. She gave other support, a lot of it, and the book could not have been written without her.

Kat Crawford, critique partner and friend extra-ordinaire, provided excellent help and support whenever I asked since this project began in 2002.

Author's Note

This story is based on the true story of Monica Moore, who assumes God has given her a green light to move ahead until he gives her a red light. As you read you may say, "This couldn't possibly be true." But it is true. It's unusual, but most events actually happened and the rest are based in fact. Names of people and places have been changed to protect the identity of anyone involved.

—1—

CULTURE SHOCK

Sunday, June 11, 2006, Chengdu, China

Why did I insist on making this trip? Sixteen-year-old Erika Slade blinked in the morning light on the Air China jet and glared at her snoring seatmate. He inhaled with his mouth closed, held his breath for at least ten seconds, and exhaled with a great whoosh of air that flapped his lips out.

"Cabbage breath," she said. "Disgusting."

After the other members of their group disembarked in Beijing, a Chinese man took the seat next to her for their connecting flights. Soon volunteers for the English as a Second Language China Group (ESLCG) would be scattered all over the country. She already detested the language barrier because she could not give the man even a polite hello.

Stiff from the 12-hour flight from Chicago, Erika shifted in her seat and tried to remember the reason she agreed to this trip. Deep down she knew she couldn't bear to be apart from her seatmate on the right, 68-year-old Monica Moore.

Erika would never forget Monica's kind face and loving words back in January when she found clean, dry clothes for Erika and her twin brother Billy and fixed hot chocolate. After their mother had thrown them out of the house, a cop brought them to the Hope Shelter.

"I'm glad I just happened to be here, delivering used clothes I collected," Monica said after she listened to the twins' story and helped them negotiate terms with Mom at home. Since then, she stayed in touch and answered their every phone call. One time she even drove to their house to settle their argument with Mom.

"You're like another grandma," Erika said.

Monica wrapped her in a warm, lingering hug and murmured, "I need another grandchild."

When the small blonde lady with blue eyes announced she was going to China, Erika begged to go along and her friend arranged everything. But no one had warned her that foul smells came with the trip.

"Cabbage breath," Erika repeated. "Eeww!" He opened his eyes for a moment. She dug in her red straw bag for a can of breath mints and motioned for him to take one, but he shook his head. Pointing to the little candy box, then to him, she placed a mint in her mouth and pushed the tin closer to his face.

He bowed his head slightly and accepted a mint. Then he twisted away from her and snored as if he'd never been interrupted.

"I could have saved a mint if I knew he was

gonna turn away." She started to close the lid.

Monica chuckled and reached for her own breath mint at the same time the "fasten seatbelts" sign went on. "Ah, we're almost there."

Erika stuck the mints back in her bag as she glimpsed the runway below. Her stomach churned. China! Land that Monica loved. But would she?

The jet grumbled into its descent toward the Chengdu airport. The teenager whisked a rubber band off her wrist and tied her long auburn hair into a tight ponytail. She linked arms with Monica as the plane rolled to a stop on the tarmac half a world away from their hometown, Seneca, Kansas.

Cabbage man spit his mint into his hand and shoved it into his pocket as he moved down the aisle toward the exit.

"He must not like mint." Erika's eyes followed the yellow happy face sticker on his computer case until it disappeared into the crowd at the exit.

Monica smiled at her young friend. "Many Chinese have cavities so sugar makes their teeth hurt."

"Oh, I'm sorry. I wasn't thinking about his teeth, just my nose." Erika cringed at the thought of his breath and recoiled at the hot, humid air filtering around them at the exit door. Smells of jet fuel and rotten eggs in the heavy air attacked her nose and the wind kicked up clouds of dust. "Oh lovely! Just lovely! I didn't know it'd smell like sour garbage here."

"It's bad in the big cities." Monica's eyes sparkled. Erika guessed that her friend barely heard her complaints.

Erika peered into the heat waves shimmering off the tarmac and realized she could barely see the buildings about a block away. "Ummm... .Wh-wh-where's the terminal?"

"Oh, we have to ride the shuttle bus to the terminal."

Diesel fumes and bugs blew in the window of the battered yellow bus. Erika grabbed the handles as the driver made a fast turn and zoomed for the station at top speed.

Monica leaned back, closed her eyes and smiled. She didn't seem to notice the bugs, the dust, the fumes or the fast ride. "Ah, China! Lord, let me tell everyone that I meet about you." She opened her eyes and greeted each person who walked past her seat with a smile that beat a Jack-o-lantern's, seriously, it was that big.

Erika let go of the handles when the bus stopped and smoothed her hair. *Since I'm here I might as well try to like the place*, she thought. "Hey, Monica," she said, "can you send some of your love my way? Right now I just don't feel any."

"You'll be okay when we get into our classes," Monica said. "Let's go get our luggage." She was halfway down the aisle before Erika could gather her carry-ons.

In the terminal, they passed through customs and headed for the baggage pick-up. "Thanks for the suitcase, Monica. The wheels make a huge difference, and red is my favorite color." Her smile probably looked as fake as a beauty queen's wish for world peace, but Erika vowed to try hard to please the little lady next to her.

"Red's my favorite color too." Monica lifted her own red-wheeled suitcase off the rickety conveyor belt clattering past them. "China University, here we come."

Reality settled in, driving Erika to a mild sense of panic as she rolled her suitcase behind Monica toward the waiting area. All the people speaking Chinese made her insides shiver and a tight band squeezed her chest. What if she never caught the fundamentals of the Chinese language? She could get lost in this crazy country and nobody would find her.

Erika could never tell her excited friend about the fear gripping her body and mind, making her hands tremble on her bags. Stifling air and the stench of a man's unwashed body, in a compact space, assaulted her nose. Her unexpected panic mixed with the uncommon smell caused her bowels to lurch.

"I wrote Professor Bing that he'd recognize me by my red jacket and blonde hair." Monica broke into an excited grin as she spied a group of waiting Chinese. "Oh, that must be him in the group over there." An average-sized man in a beige sports shirt and brown slacks started toward them.

Every muscle tightened on Erika's body and she caught her breath as another wave of nausea swept over her. *I am not afraid. I will not throw up*, she commanded herself.

Monica shook the man's hand. "You're Professor Bing?"

"Yes." He shook hands with both Americans.

"I'm Monica Moore and this is Erika Slade." *I've already forgotten the instructions Monica gave us last week on greeting the Chinese,* she thought.

"Welcome to China! I represent China University and our first volunteer English program." Professor Bing waved the rest of his group over. "These officials have come to welcome you." Erika crossed her arms and made a smile that was more fake than the first one. She smelled Bengay on Professor Bing and choked back her vomit yet a third time.

"Oh, I appreciate such a large welcome." Monica introduced Erika and shook hands with the six people who smiled and spoke all at once.

Erika made an effort to greet everyone, but she could only stare at Professor Bing's bald spot, which reflected the bright ceiling lights. She willed the butterflies to stop playing tag in her tummy.

— 2 —

ME? IN CHINA?

"China University is very honored to have you come from America." Professor Bing rubbed his elbow and waved his hand toward a tall, skinny man. "This is Mr. Xun, Party Secretary at China University."

Erika gulped. *Woohoo!* she thought. *Back in America, Monica said the party secretary is the most powerful person at the University, and I can't believe I'm standing next to him*.

A shock of prematurely gray hair drooped over one eye as Mr. Xun bent from his waist. Erika wondered if he had even a fingernail's worth of fat to pinch. A little ditty flew through her head, "Zun, Zun, Zun. The leader man. And X-u-n spells Zun in this crazy world."

Then came Dr. Dong, the college president, looking scholarly in round steel-rimmed glasses perched on his long nose.

Dr. Du, the gorgeous vice president in a blue summer suit, wore her hair in a tight bun with an ivory chopstick poking out at a sharp angle. Erika wondered if it was a real chopstick. Maybe Dr. Du carried the other one in that lime green bag of hers. Did she eat with them at every meal? What about soup?

Erika totally missed the three other names. There was no way she could possibly keep everyone straight.

"It is 9:00 a.m. already and our trip will take eight or nine hours. We must leave right after breakfast." Professor Bing gripped the handle of Monica's suitcase and turned toward the outside doors to the van.

Monica handed him her jacket, but when the professor reached for her purse she said, "Thanks for offering, but my purse has my passport and many important papers."

Erika crossed both arms over her own bag and no one offered to carry it. Three of the men grabbed for the other luggage and after a bit of tugging, each man carried a piece or two.

"We will eat breakfast." Mr. Xun set out for the dining area in a long-legged lope and the women scurried after him.

Erika needed a trip to the ladies' room, but would she be safe? She decided she had no choice but to take the risk. "Excuse me, where's the rest-room?"

Mr. Xun craned his neck and looked at her, but said nothing.

"I'll go with you," Monica said and grabbed Erika's hand. She chatted and followed the signs without seeming to notice Erika's silence. "Here it is." The two friends joined the other women entering the large, dimly lit room with dark concrete walls.

Erika gasped and clutched her hands over her nose. "What's that awful smell? Oh, no! I'm going to be sick!" She sprinted across the old tile floor to the huge wastebasket by the hand dryers.

"I'm so sorry you don't feel well." Monica fished a bottle of water and a nausea pill out of her bag. Erika rinsed her mouth with a little water and then downed the pill.

Monica opened the door to the middle stall and motioned. "Here, use this one."

"Do they have seat cov—?" Erika clapped a hand over her mouth and burst into tears. "Is this seriously the toilet? What did they do? Just put a sink in the middle of the floor? Do I sit on it or what? I'll get some kind of disease." She fought the desire to bolt out of there and get on a plane for home.

"Oh, Erika, honey, you're all nervous and you're making yourself sick. Listen, you squat over the little sink, and always put your tissues in the basket because the pipes are old and you can't flush anything down the drain."

Erika fumbled with the cubicle door latch as she tried to wrap her mind around the idea. She heaved a huge sigh just as a small woman with a gold barrette in her short hair and a toothy grin appeared next to them with a basket of mud-colored paper.

"Here's the tissue vendor." Monica held up two

fingers and the woman handed her two wads of paper. "It looks like ground up cardboard, doesn't it?" She gave one to Erika with a smile.

"No gentle Charmin here." Soft white tissue suddenly seemed a distant memory. Was it really yesterday she'd used it at home?

The vendor held up one finger and Monica handed her a Chinese bill, informing Erika, "one Yuan is equal to 12 cents in American money." She stepped into the first stall.

Other women and children used the third stall or leaned against the concrete partition to await their turn. Some didn't bother to flush and the eye-watering odors multiplied.

"Are all the bathrooms in China gonna be like this?" Erika asked as she left the cubical.

Monica patted her arm. "Most aren't as nice as this, but soon you won't think a thing about it."

"No. Believe me. I'll never get used to this." They washed their hands at the row of sinks against the far wall and fled the stench.

In the dining room, Erika looked up at the Chinese lanterns covering bare bulbs, glowing softly over dark tables and chairs. A few photos of the Forbidden City and other tourist spots were tacked to the beige walls. Dr. Du motioned to chairs on either side of her. "Come sit down."

Erika noted the chopstick still in Dr. Du's hair, but saw no sign of its mate. *Maybe she saves the ivory ones for special occasions*, she thought.

The nausea pill kicked in, finally. "My grandpa used to say, 'I'm so hungry I could eat a horse,' and

I feel that way right now."

The server arched his eyebrows and responded in broken English, "So sorry, but we have not horses on the menu."

"No, really, I don't want to eat a horse... ."

Professor Bing interrupted and rambled in Chinese, evidently explaining what Erika meant. When the server began bowing and chuckling, she giggled behind her hand and everyone else laughed with her.

She ate the rice and eggs the server brought in big bowls, family style. The adults who spoke English made pleasant conversation and interpreted for the less fluent. Erika resisted the urge to gulp down the tea from her tiny cup, but she ended up asking for three refills.

The group finished their meal and gathered outside by the van. Mr. Xun opened the front passenger door and motioned for Erika and Monica to climb in. "You may have the seat of honor in the front seat, next to the door, and Erika will sit in the middle."

"Thank you so much, but since there are no seatbelts, we would rather sit back there," Monica said, pointing behind the driver.

Mr. Xun opened the door and Monica hopped onto the second seat. She slid with her bags all the way to the opposite door. Erika sat in the middle, with Dr. Du next to the open door.

"Ah, it's air-conditioned! God is merciful." Erika leaned back on the brown vinyl and released any leftover nausea and fear into the chilled air. After all, they could all be in a rickshaw like the old fashioned one she'd seen near the airport, with Mr. Xun trotting along, pulling them toward Nanchong. She grinned at the thought of him in short pants and a pointy hat.

Professor Bing had introduced Mr. Liu as the substitute from a driving pool. The University hired him because the regular driver was sick. Erika shook her head, remembering the crazy-fast drive from the plane.

The airport disappeared behind them as Mr. Liu zipped onto a highway buzzing with construction. Erika pulled her hair out of the ponytail as she gazed at the farmers planting rice in a nearby field. "Look, they're using—what? A cow? To pull that thing? A rice planter?"

"That's a water buffalo," Monica answered. They watched several workers wading in the rice paddy, poking rice plants into the mud behind the buffalo.

Mr. Xun explained the road they were on in answer to Monica's quizzing. "This will be an expressway between Nanchong and Chengdu when it's finished."

Erika gazed out the window, watching the road workers cart stones along the ditch. Suddenly she gasped and exclaimed, "Those are women out there, hauling rocks. They're as old as you, Monica. No offense, but could you carry big rocks like that?"

"No, I couldn't."

Erika noted the tears in Monica's eyes and guessed she was praying for the women.

Erika glanced at Monica again and leaned forward. "So, Mr. Liu, you're a professional driver?" *Monica said professional driving is a huge business in China,* she thought.

"Yes," Mr. Liu looked over his shoulder and responded with a grin. He barely missed several workers chopping a hole in the roadbed with pick axes.

"I have a driver's license back in America," Erika said, "but I don't know how anyone drives on this road. It's so narrow and sandy. How can you stand it?"

Mr. Liu smiled, but kept his eyes on the oxcart he'd pulled behind too fast. If brakes could squeal in sand, his would have.

"When did you say this road will be finished?

"In a couple of years." Mr. Xun yawned.

Erika let her eyebrows shoot up. "Years?"

Mr. Xun nodded. "It has been ten already."

In America a project like this would take a year, she thought. She looked out the windows again, at the mob of workers in their pointed hats, stooping over huge boulders and piles of dirt. There were no trucks or bulldozers in sight. Fine sand collected on the outside van windows and slid down the glass. She licked her lips and tasted grit. Unbelievable! Monica probably didn't notice the dust on her skirt.

Erika opened her mouth to ask a question, but Mr. Xun spoke first.

"We usually take naps in the afternoon. Would you like one?"

"Naps? Umm... . Sure, I guess. I mean I didn't get much sleep last night anyway." Erika scrunched her five-foot-nine-inch body into resting position and laid her head on Monica's shoulder. "I'm glad you're short and I can put some of your space to good use." She grinned up at her mentor.

Monica smoothed Erika's hair and kissed her forehead.

Erika beamed when Dr. Du scooted closer to the door.

"Thank you, Dr. Du. You're very kind," Monica said.

The pretty woman's face broke into a wide smile.

Almost everyone else had dropped off to sleep. Erika frowned as images of Daddy appeared at the edges of her mind and flitted through her memory. Would she ever stop missing him? Her mind flashed to her younger years when she napped with him in the green recliner at home. She knew she couldn't think of him or she'd break down and cry for sure.

Monica patted Mr. Liu's shoulder. "I won't sleep because I want to see what this part of China is like. I've never driven through the area by car."

"Where do you get your energy, Monica?" Erika flashed back to the 12-hour trip from Chicago. Monica stayed busy reading, praying or chatting with other passengers most of the night. And now she had too many questions about China to take a nap.

Erika dozed for a few minutes and awoke to hear Monica talking with Driver Liu. How could anyone understand his broken English?

"This is such a beautiful countryside." Monica asked many questions about the houses, the crops and tier planting, and ended with, "What do you think, Mr. Liu."

Mr. Liu answered every question, often with waving hands or a glance back. Several times he almost ran off the road, but grabbed the steering wheel just in time.

Erika shifted her legs and kept her eyes closed.

While the Chinese passengers slept, Erika listened to Monica's whispered prayers for everyone inside the van and out, for the people in the fields, and for the country of China.

Did the woman ever quit? Next thing you know, she would claim China for Christ.

— 3 —

CITY TO CITY

Monica had already claimed China for Christ on the plane. A million times at least. "Everywhere the sole of your foot shall tread, that shall I give you," she quoted from the Bible. Erika's head buzzed.

She glanced at Monica. "I wish I could text message Billy," she whispered. "I'm already going crazy without my cell phone."

She pulled her laptop out of her bag. "Maybe I can send him an instant message."

"But wouldn't he be asleep?" Monica whispered back. "They're 15 hours behind us." She checked her watch. "It's three here, so... ."

"It's twelve there. He's probably asleep because he has to work tomorrow." Erika slumped in the seat and started to shove her laptop back into her bag. "I know, I'll email him. But who could I write to have him look for an email? I know, Grandma."

Hey Bro-B, we made it to the Chengdu airport this morn'in. It's ridiculously hot and dusty here, like home. The air smells funny and the bathrooms are disgusting.

I was soooo nervous this morning that I upchucked in the bathroom. You wouldn't believe this place! It's got like all these strange smells with people babbling Chinese and swarming in like every direction. Crazy. It's awesome lol!

I'm homesick, At least I think am. Kinda, well maybe just a lil. So anyway I mean I don't miss Mom. Not at all, but I sure do miss you lots, Bro J!

Me and Monica talked bout why you stayed back with Mom when you could've came with us. Did ya think ya should take care of her or somethin? We prayed for ya on the plane ya know? We prayed that you could make it through mom's crazy rages. Every time I think bout ya stayin home alone and how much mom hurts us, it makes me sad Bro L. Is she worse w/o me there? I sure hope not L!

It sorta feels like I've been gone foooor-ever and you're just part of my imagination. I don't even remember whatcha look like right now L.

Maybe Daddy missed us like this when he was in Iraq? Maybe, just maybe!

I keep thinking about Dad. I almost cried because I miss him soooo much bro. I couldn't even think about his funeral. I want to strangle those Iraqis that shot down his helicopter!

Write back soon, b/c I really miss ya Bro L.

Love ya - Erika

She snapped her notebook shut and quickly opened it again. "I have to email Grandma and tell her I emailed Billy." She quickly typed a short note.

Hey, Grandma! We made it to China! Such a stinky place, but Monica is sure I'll love it after I get used to everything. I hope it happens fast because right now I think I'm in the weirdest place on the planet.

I had to email Billy because I couldn't bring my cell phone and he's probably asleep so I can't IM him. Would you call him in the morning and tell him I sent him an email? Thanks, Grams, you're the best grandma I've ever had. I know, you're the only one because Mom doesn't know where her parents are.

I love you lots! Miss you! Write! Erika

She gazed out the window at nothing in particular. Monica had said they couldn't send emails except from the port in their hotel lobby. She wished for her CD player and her favorite Jeremy Camp CD.

Once again Erika wondered why she'd insisted on this trip. But she knew the answer: Monica.

Such a sweet lady. It felt good just sitting next to her now. In fact, it felt 100 percent better than sitting at home without her.

She opened her laptop again and moved the cursor to the end of her last sentence.

> *I don't have anything else to do so I'll add to my email. I hope ya don't mind reading all these words.*
>
> *Being with Monica is mega peaceful and relaxing. I think she really likes me! All these China problems are worth it if I can just be with her! I'm soooo happy she listened to me when I begged her to let me come along. I just wish ya were here with me L! She's told me a million times that she doesn't usually take such young Christians with her. I counted up and we made our decision to turn our lives over to Jesus six weeks ago! Isn't that sweet?!?!? Like Daddy used to say, time flies when you're having fun. Getting acquainted with Jesus is definitely cool.*
>
> *Right now, we're in a van headed for Nanchong (I think that's how you spell it) and China University. Mr. Xun (Zun), the Communist Party Secretary at China University (!!!!) said we'll get there at like sixish. We have to show him lotsa respect and stuff because he's some important guy.*
>
> *Thank God for air conditioning, or else I may have to just die! Mr. Xun says it's like 104 degrees outside. Isn't that nuts?*

Later, Bro, unless I choke to death in a pile of road dust lol. E

She deleted the former closing and typed in, *Luv ya! Erika*

She was putting away her laptop when Monica shouted, "Mr. Liu, look out!" and a loud "bang" shook the van. Erika flew across the seat, almost into Dr. Du's lap. She forgot to apologize when Mr. Liu slumped in his seat and the van careened toward the edge of the road.

"God help us!" Monica prayed in a loud voice.

"I've got it." Professor Bing grabbed the steering wheel and fought for control. With his left foot he reached past Mr. Liu's legs and applied pressure to the brakes. Erika clung to Monica until the van stopped on the sandy road edge.

"Mr. Liu, can you hear me?" Monica leaned forward and checked for a pulse on his neck. "He's breathing okay and his heartbeat is strong. Oh! Be careful of the glass. It's everywhere." She carefully pulled shards off her clothes.

"What happened?" The men in the back seat looked dazed and held their heads.

Monica pointed to an SUV stopped on the road in front of them. "That car came flying out of the side street and plowed into our van." Erika looked down at her shaking hands and tried not to cry, but tears slid down her face anyway. Monica carefully hugged the teen's shoulders as she picked glass from Erika's clothes and hair.

Dr. Du handed her a tissue from her purse and carefully removed the shards on her own clothes. "I wish he had watched where he was going."

Slowly, Mr. Liu sat up and groaned. "My head." He fumbled for the door latch, but didn't open the door. "An accident, and it wasn't my fault," he mumbled. "I'll lose my job for this."

"Let's get out and check the damage." Mr. Xun and Professor Bing stepped out and opened all of the doors except the one behind Monica. "This door will not open. Look at that big dent. And the glass in the window is completely gone." Mr. Xun yanked on the handle again. "Are you okay, Miss Monica?"

"I seem to be okay." Monica rubbed her neck.

"Be sure to tell us if your neck starts to hurt." Mr. Xun stuck his head through the window and peered into her eyes. "I will look into your eyes to see if you are in shock or if you have a concussion." After a moment he said, "No, both pupils are the same size."

The two men in the back seat still looked dazed.

"Unbelievable! Your heads must have smacked something really really hard." Erika stared at the huge bruises beginning to rise on their foreheads.

"I wish we had some ice to put on those bumps." Monica looked around as if she expected an ice machine to rise out of the sand. She didn't seem to notice the scorching heat.

Little trickles of sweat started at Erika's hairline and traced through the dust on her cheeks. She couldn't think of anything else, just her misery at the moment.

"In China we never take anyone to the hospital unless he is seriously injured." Professor Bing rubbed his elbow.

Mr. Liu looks seriously injured, Erika thought, but she swallowed her comment and wished for a drink of water.

Monica held up a white plastic box. "I'm a nurse. I have my first-aid kit." She and Professor Bing helped the two men find a seat in the shade of the van and checked their injuries. Mr. Xun led Mr. Liu to the same shade and checked him over.

Monica gave the men some Tylenol and Mr. Xun handed each one a bottle of water. They leaned their heads against the van, eyes closed.

Mr. Xun walked around it, opened the hood and looked underneath. "The van looks drivable after we fix the broken window."

"I think there's a piece of cardboard under the back seat." Professor Bing went to find it and forced it into the grooves where the glass had been. Dr. Du and Erika collected the glass shards in a small box they found tumbling along the road in the wind.

Monica and Professor Bing talked to the other driver, whose only injury appeared to be a small scratch on his nose. His SUV had a crumpled hood and right front fender, but they decided it was drivable. Erika stood behind Monica and listened as the man seemed to apologize in Chinese. Professor Bing responded again and again, sometimes gruffly. Erika stepped closer and caught a whiff of the man's breath.

Drunk!

They exchanged personal information and the group climbed back into the van. Professor Bing slid behind the wheel. "Mr. Liu, I will drive until we are sure you feel well." The driver scooted to the middle front seat and let out a sigh as his shoulders relaxed.

Erika hid her relief over not having to ride next to Professor Bing and his Bengay.

The two men in the back seat gave weak smiles when Dr. Du seemed to ask them if they felt okay. She interpreted when they said in Chinese that they felt better.

"Whew! That was close." Erika sipped her water and pulled her lip-gloss out of her bag. But her hands felt gritty and there was no place to wash them. She decided to skip the lip-gloss.

"I could lose my job," Mr. Liu repeated.

"The accident wasn't your fault," Monica assured him. "You shouldn't lose your job if it wasn't your fault."

Leave it to Monica to find something encouraging to say to this wild driver.

"I will see that he doesn't lose his job." Mr. Xun passed out more bottles of water from a sports bag between his feet on the van floor. Mr. Liu's big smile made his ears rise half an inch.

Monica downed half the bottle before she took a breath. "Thanks. This'll wash the dust out of my throat."

Mr. Xun checked his watch and pointed. "Professor Bing, we have been on the road a long time. We will stop at that restaurant and I will buy food."

"Food! I'm starving. I'll take a cheeseburger with the works and fries. And a giant Coke, please." Erika giggled, but Monica frowned and whispered that Erika should accept whatever was offered.

Everyone waited in the van while Mr. Xun went inside. Professor Bing pulled a tube of Bengay out of his pocket and applied some to his elbow. "I have Bursitis," he said, replacing the cap.

Frown lines appeared between Monica's brows and compassion filled her eyes as she said, "I'm sorry. May I pray for you?"

The professor's eyeballs seemed about ready to pop out of his head, but he shook his head yes. Monica laid her hand on his arm and prayed for his Bursitis to disappear. *Professor Bing looks like he's seen a ghost,* Erika thought.

Mr. Xun brought back a bag filled with pouches about the size of a small lemon. When he handed her four, she discovered they were made from what looked like noodles with meat and vegetables all rolled up inside.

"Oh, Jaiaozi. I love these." Monica handed some to the men behind her. Professor Bing drove with one hand while he ate a couple of the dumplings.

"I'm starved!" Erika wolfed down the J-blobs and could have eaten twice what Mr. Xun gave her. As she swallowed, the Asian aftertaste made her think she'd rather have something like a Big Mac and fries. She hadn't realized how much she would miss American food...until now.

No one said anything for a few minutes. Mr. Liu dozed, his head bobbing in rhythm with the bouncing van.

Erika couldn't resist asking, "How much longer till we get there?" She really wished she had her cell phone. How could she possibly survive without a phone for two whole months?

"About an hour," Professor Bing said as he negotiated a sharp turn behind some barriers. "We lost forty-five minutes with the accident. We will get there around seven."

Erika repressed a sigh. Her legs had turned to pretzels, or at least it felt that way. She thought of asking Professor Bing to stop the van and let her out to run for a while, but jogging would be a killer in this heat. She chomped her lip.

More junk and obstacles flew past as Erika stared out the window. Little kids playing in the dirt, old people on bikes, more women working on the road. She gazed at the foreign landscape. "Look at those cows tied to the farmer's fence next to his house. I wanna pet 'em." When would this crazy hot trip end? She applied lip-gloss and scraped at the gritty dirt on her face and hands again. *I hope this new shade of make-up called "Sand" complements my complexion*, she thought.

* * *

Finally Mr. Xun announced, "Miss Monica and Erika, we have arrived in Nanchong."

"Welcome to China University!" Professor

Bing beamed and waved his arm as they drove onto a street lined with flowers of every color imaginable. Erika feasted her eyes on the lovely blooms and inhaled their fragrance as it flowed through the air conditioner into the van.

"I'm so glad to be here." Monica sniffed the sweet air and commented on the trees and neat walkways.

Professor Bing pointed out the English Department building. "Your classes will meet there."

"Cool! That building is huge!" Erika leaned over Monica's lap to see the top.

"Yes, every student has to study *written* English in China, but your team will teach *oral* English, Professor Bing said. "We need a large building to provide classrooms for all the students."

"What a lovely campus!" Monica's eyes sparkled as the van pulled in front of a hotel.

"This is the Guesthouse, where you will stay." The professor cut the engine.

"Who are those people over there, waving at us?" Monica waved back.

"They are teachers, students and anyone else who wants to learn English in your classes. They have been waiting here to greet you and make you feel welcome."

"Greet us? How long have they waited?"

"They have waited all afternoon. They are very glad you are here." He and Mr. Xun got out and opened the van doors. Then he made a little speech to the crowd. In English he said, "This is Miss Monica Moore from America and her friend

Erika Slade. Miss Monica has come to teach English this summer, and Erika will be her assistant."

Erika rolled her eyes and thought, *Wouldn't these people already know this?*

He launched into a longer speech in Chinese and from their expressions and the professor's body language, Erika guessed he was explaining the delay, the damaged van and the bruised university officials.

Monica smiled and greeted every one of the fifty or so people. Erika thought about following her mentor's example, but she just couldn't. Maybe it would be easier tomorrow when classes started. She leaned against the van.

What she wouldn't give to see Billy come walking across the lawn. Or Daddy. She missed him so much. She gave in to her weepy feelings and let a few tears fall. Then she prayed that God would make her red, puffy eyes disappear. Monica had said God was concerned about every little thing, and she didn't want to explain why she'd been crying.

— 4 —

THE HAIRCUT

"Here you are!" Erika jumped when Monica and Professor Bing came around the corner of the van. Fortunately, they didn't seem to notice any tear-stains.

Monica suppressed a yawn and checked her watch. "It's after eight and we start classes tomorrow."

"I will walk you to your rooms." Professor Bing started to lift their luggage out of the van and suddenly stopped. Then he rubbed his elbow and flexed his arm. "My elbow does not hurt any more." His face contorted into a frown and he looked at his elbow again.

"Thank you, Jesus." Monica's smile lit up the entire area and Erika clapped and did a little happy dance. Professor Bing just rubbed his elbow.

A passing college student glanced curiously from Erika to Professor Bing to Monica and back again.

"Tell him what happened." Monica interrupted her little dance of joy. Professor Bing's eyes darted around the parking lot as he spoke a few words in Chinese. The student looked as if it were his turn to see a ghost. He eyed the elbow without touching it, probably out of respect for his professor. Then he bowed. Erika presumed he volunteered to help carry the luggage because Professor Bing tipped his head slightly and handed him two suitcases.

The kid stared at Erika's hair hanging halfway down her back. Maybe he'd never seen auburn hair before. Or maybe he thought she was cute. Erika smiled at him and he jumped and looked away, as if he hadn't realized he was staring.

They climbed the steps to the third floor and walked down the dim hallway. College Man set down the luggage and started back down the hall. Monica called, "Come to our classes in the English Building tomorrow."

Professor Bing seemed to explain the invitation in Chinese, but College Man shook his head. "He is busy all day because he carries a heavy class load," the professor explained. Monica and Erika waved at his back as he retreated.

Professor Bing swung Monica's door open and Erika sniffed the stale heat from the room. No air conditioning. She'd melt for sure.

"This is lovely." Monica inspected the standard beige walls, two twin beds with bamboo mattresses for coolness, and pillows filled with soybeans. "This dresser will be just right for my clothes." She checked the bathroom. "All right, a bathtub. Thank you, God."

Erika flashed to Monica's stories of how a knock

came often on her door late at night and the visitor whispered, "I want to hear about Jesus." Monica always invited the person in and shared a pamphlet called *Step Up To Life.* The seeker nearly always made a decision to accept Christ's love and guidance for his life, and a baptism followed. Without the tub in her room, Monica had to find one for the baptism or simply pour water over the new convert's head.

"Your room is exactly like mine," Monica said as Professor Bing opened the door between her room and Erika's.

It smells the same too. "Except I have a shower rather than a tub." Erika smiled. "Thank you, Professor Bing, for such a nice room."

"You are welcome, Erika. If you need anything, let me know."

"Thank you."

"Your meals will be prepared in the dining room downstairs." Professor Bing rubbed his elbow again and looked startled. He probably forgot it didn't hurt anymore. "Is there anything else you need right now?"

"Yes." Monica twizzled the ends of her shoulder-length hair. "I am desperate for a haircut. I didn't have time to get it cut in America because I went to a conference last week."

"We have a barbershop in this building. It is this way."

He started to lead the way when Erika said, "Is it okay if I stay here and take a shower?"

"Oh, certainly. Eat those protein bars in my bag if you're hungry." Monica set her bag on the desk next to Erika.

"Food! Yes! I can't believe how hungry I am all of a sudden."

"Drink the bottled water, too, and remember not to drink out of the faucets." Monica hugged her young friend. "Welcome to China, my dear."

The frazzled teen leaned down and rested her forehead on her adoptive grandmother's shoulder. Erika knew anything bad she said about this horrible country would hurt the older lady's feelings.

Monica picked up her purse.

She's the only good part of this trip. Erika stepped sidewise to allow the others out the door.

"We will not be long," the professor said as he followed Monica into the hall.

Erika rushed to the shower before the door clicked shut, eager to wash the first layer of China off her skin.

* * *

Five minutes later, Professor Bing and Monica stepped into the barbershop. "I will talk to the manager." The professor gingerly stepped over piles of black hair on the floor from the day's haircuts and headed for the reception area. He came back grinning. "They have never cut a woman's hair, or blonde hair, but everything should work out." He led the way to the third chair down and introduced Monica to a small, thin woman. The ladies shook hands and smiled.

"Sit down please." Monica soon discovered that this standard phrase was the only English the woman knew.

"Okay, please tell her I want just the ends cut off." Monica settled under the huge plastic cape. Professor Bing interpreted and the barber picked up her scissors.

Monica glanced at the woman's hands. "Professor Bing, her hands are shaking! Please talk to her and help reassure her." He started a conversation in Chinese and soon the woman began to smile. Eventually her hands stopped shaking.

Professor Bing started a conversation with the manager outside the door. Monica felt her hair falling away in the back. The barber was cutting the back short like a man's! Panic filled her. Was something lost in the translation? Professor Bing still talked to the manager, too far away to hear her if she called him.

Soon Barber Woman stopped her work and removed the cape. Monica looked in the mirror by the chair. "Lord, please help me not to laugh," she said out loud, knowing the woman couldn't understand English. "What a sight!" Barber Woman had barely touched the front of Monica's hair. She looked like a blonde Cousin IT from *The Addams Family*. Monica ran her fingers over the short stubble from one ear to the other in the back. "I look like a horse with two manes. Oh, thank you! Thank you! I appreciate your help!" Professor Bing came back and interpreted the part Monica wanted the barber to hear. His shoulders shook as he struggled to keep from laughing out loud.

"I am glad you like the work I did. One Yuan please." Professor Bing interpreted again.

He didn't interpret Monica's response, though: "twelve cents? Is that the going rate in China? I pay $25 at home."

Outside the barbershop, Monica and Professor Bing laughed until they could hardly walk. "I can't teach the class like this." Monica wiped her tears.

"Come to our apartment. My wife Cao Yu and I will try to fix your hair." He hiccupped another chuckle as they rounded the corner and started up the stairs.

The humor of the situation stayed with them during their climb up seven flights in the heat and dim light from the single bulb at the top of the last landing.

Cao Yu greeted her unexpected guest with smiles and bows that put Monica at ease. Her flawless complexion showed tiny smile lines around her mouth and eyes. Monica guessed she must be about 45 years old, a few years younger than Professor Bing who looked to be about 55. She wore her hair parted high up, almost in the middle, hanging to her shoulders. Her pink shirt brought out her skin tones and cast a rosy glow to her cheeks, even without makeup.

Monica relaxed in the air-conditioned room, nicely furnished with a dark brown sofa, beige chairs and a table against white walls. Jade figurines and antique fans accessorized the end tables and soft light gleamed from ornate light fixtures hung high up on the walls. Decorated tiles made an easy-to-clean floor.

"I look like a man in the back and a woman on the sides," Monica said and laughed.

"We are glad you are not upset," Professor Bing said.

"This will be a great story to tell the grandchildren," Monica said, still chuckling.

The professor interpreted for Yu and they all laughed together.

Husband and wife conferred in Chinese for a couple of minutes. Monica assumed he told Yu about the trip because he pointed to his elbow and flexed his arm as if to show his wife that it didn't hurt. Then he pointed to his watch to indicate the passing of time and asked Monica in English, "How old is Erika?

Soon he turned to Monica with a smile. "First Yu will cook some chicken to make you feel better."

Yu interrupted him and he interpreted, "Thank you for helping my husband get rid of that stinky Bengay," and they all laughed.

"Thank you for your help, Yu. Too bad Erika isn't here to watch this haircut and taste the food."

The professor interpreted for Monica and then for Yu, "You must be sure to take some food to Erika."

Yu cooked the chicken and vegetables on her stovetop.

She doesn't have an oven, Monica thought, glancing around the tiny kitchen. She knew from past years' experience that most Chinese cook everything on the burners, with lots of fat or boiling water because they do not have ovens.

*   *   *

"This is wonderful chicken! You are a good cook." Monica expertly manipulated her chopsticks. Professor Bing interpreted and Yu smiled at the compliment. Then Yu put a big towel around Monica's shoulders and the women giggled as Professor Bing furrowed his brow, flexed his fingers and started snipping away.

In a few minutes, he handed Monica a mirror. "I had to cut your hair very short to match the back."

Monica ran her fingers through her short, short hair. "Thank you very much. Maybe I'll call you Professor Bing the barber from now on." She gazed into the mirror. "The other barber charged me 12 cents, but you were free. And Yu's chicken restaurant is the best in the city."

— 5 —

CORN KERNELS AND BAMBOO

Erika answered the knock on her door around 10 p.m., but she barely recognized the woman standing there with a dazzling grin. "Monica? Is that you? What happened to your hair?"

"Professor Bing cut it."

"But I thought you went to a barber shop."

"I'll tell you the story, but first his wife sent you some dinner." Erika wolfed down the chicken and some rice and vegetables before Monica could even finish telling the haircut story.

They laughed and laughed while Erika finger-combed Monica's hair with gel. "I almost didn't bring this," she said. "I just use a dab on the front to keep it from frizzing around my face, but it did the curly cue anyway today."

Then the conversation turned to the next day and those all-important English classes. "Remember, that's why we're here." Monica glanced in the mirror to see what Erika had done. "Oh, you're very creative. Will you do it for me again?"

"Sure."

"The rest of the team from America will be here around midnight." Monica patted Erika's clean-from-the-shower hair. "We'll meet in the dining room around seven thirty in the morning and go from there. I know you've had a rough start, but you'll love China."

Erika studied the Pale-Pink Moonbeam nail polish she'd applied after her shower. "I keep wondering what I'm doing so far from home This is the weirdest place I've ever been."

"I'm glad you came with me, though. We make a great team, but you'd better get to bed now." Monica glanced one more time in the mirror and patted her hair. "By the way, I called Charlotte in America and let her know we made it okay. What would we do without her prayers?" Monica started toward her own room.

"I can't believe Charlotte is really 90." Erika took one last glance at her nail polish and winced as she slid over the mattress that was covered only by a sheet. "What kind of mattress is this?"

"It's bamboo, for coolness. You'll feel the difference on these hot nights." Monica ran her fingers through her hair for the umpteenth time.

"Two months of no air conditioner and a bamboo mattress. I hope I make it," Erika whined.

"You'll make it. Charlotte is praying for us, and so are a lot of other people."

"I really like Charlotte." Erika smiled. "She makes me laugh because she's so small, but she moves fast and talks fast."

"Charlotte insisted that I memorize Bible verses when she helped me as a new Christian, and now I'm glad because I can quote them any time." Monica glanced at her watch. "Oh, I ordered a telephone for my room. They said it would take three or four days, and I thought, 'Long enough to install microphones.'"

"That doesn't worry you, though."

"No, I make sure the listener on the other end hears about Jesus." Monica grinned as she opened her door and blew Erika a goodnight kiss. "I'm here to tell people about Jesus, and if they send me home, I'll know I told everyone I could about Him in the time I had."

"And you'll take me home with you… . Goodnight, Monica."

The sound of Monica's running bath water trickled through the thin walls as Erika flipped to Psalm 91 in her Bible. Tomorrow Monica would ask her to recite what she'd memorized. She glanced at the picture of the Great Wall hanging above her bed and quoted, "He that dwelleth in the secret place of the Most High shall abide under the shadow of the almighty… ."

She opened her laptop and added a post script to Billy's message she'd started that afternoon.

PS: There was no place to send the email I wrote ya this afternoon. And I'm so bored I think I'll just add to it.

I keep wonderin how I got to China. I

can already hear ya sayin it, "Monica." Well, you're right, she's the only reason. She's a sweet lady and totally loves everybody! She keeps saying she wants to tell every Chinese person about Jesus and I definitely believe her.

We had an accident in the van. Some drunk guy ran into us, but everyone's okay. Monica talked to him and gave him a Step Up To Life in Chinese, just like she does with everybody. I wanted to kick him in the pants lol. But she's always so loving J!

Stay close to Pastor Chuck. He'll help ya deal with Mom and everything. I'll be home in two months, unless I dry up and blow away lol. I'm missin ya like crazy bro!

Hit me back with a message. From the best twin sister you'll ever have (not to mention the only :).

Love ya, Erika.

She flipped off the light and curled into a ball. *I didn't realize what it would be like so far from home*. She pulled a handful of hair over her face as part of her nightly ritual and sniffed the sweet smell. The clock ticked. Then it hit her: Without Monica she would be like that lost kitten mewing for its mother she'd seen in the street last week. Erika craved to be near Monica, regardless. For Monica's sake she'd stay in China. And go to sleep right now. After she'd cried a little. Finally she could weep for her lost father, and for Billy so far away. The corn kernel stuffing didn't absorb tears the same as polyester filling at home.

* * *

Monica checked on Erika after her bath and found the beautiful girl sound asleep in a sliver of moonlight. "Oooh, she's been crying," Monica whispered, bending closer, observing the puffy, red eyes. "Father, thank you for this precious child. Please bless her with your peace. Comfort her homesickness," she prayed softly and placed a gentle kiss on Erika's temple. She moved the lipgloss and Bible to the bedside stand.

— 6 —

GETTING STARTED

Tuesday, June 15, 2006

The day started hot in Nanchong at 90 degrees and 90 percent humidity, with no air-conditioning. Erika checked her watch. *Tuesday, day three in China, at 6:30 a.m. One hour till breakfast*. She frowned and cringed at the thought of eye-watering smells, the heat, the dust and dirt everywhere. *China is a nightmare come true,* she thought.

Why had she agreed to this trip? Could she endure one more day of strange people, the strange language? Could she keep her opinions to herself for two whole months? Erika resolved once more to stay with Monica, regardless. She would not act like Lyda, her 12-year-old neighbor girl who always gave up at any task and went home. She couldn't think about Mom's abuse and Dad's killers, either.

The teenager heard the ping of water against the walls next door on the other side, and the neighbor's nasal voice, singing off key. *They sing in the shower here, too.* She snorted back a laugh.

She'd send Billy's email after breakfast from the port in the lobby, just like yesterday. She snapped open her laptop and reread last night's message.

Dear Bro, looks like I'm stuck here. Monica said she could arrange for me to fly home, but I know it would cost lotsa money. I think she understands why I'm homesick, but she's so excited about this stinky, dusty land that I don't want to disappoint her. I won't quit on her! And being with her helps, but I sure miss ya lots. Two months! How will I make it lol?

Ya wouldn't believe all the new things we did yesterday. I ate the food they gave us, but I'm dying for a hot dog. All they give us here is rice, combined with fish, chicken, and everything imaginable. Everything except chocolate lol J

A few of the people here, like, never change clothes or take a bath! Most do though. I changed my clothes three times yesterday and took two showers.

The students in the classes are all ages from third or fourth grade to old people. The entire campus has a wall around it and we go in through a gate with guards. Creepy :P.

Our classrooms are 15 stories up and the elevator doesn't work because the repairman is on vacation!!! Can you believe it?!?!? We climbed 15 flights of stairs three times yester-

day!!! Michael came with the team last year and he says we'll keep doing it til the repairman gets back. But basically we should plan on climbing them all freaking summer!!!

And it's so stinking hot!!! 104 degrees!

Michael is assigned to the same classroom as Monica and me. At least we have the only air-conditioned room J. That's a perk! Monica says it's a special blessing from God and she invited all the other people to our room just to cool off.

Yesterday we divided everyone into classes and helped each student choose an American name. We walked back to the Guesthouse for lunch and took naps. Then we walked back to CU (China University) and talked about American culture and government. We keep our mouths shut about the Chinese government, though.

We walked to the Guesthouse around 5:00 p.m. and some of us danced in the street with the children just for fun. They follow us everywhere and they even watch us while we eat our meals. I think they'd stay all night if we asked them.

Then we ate dinner and walked back to CU to talk away another evening lol J. The children didn't come, but we had lotsa high schoolers, college students and adults there.

How are ya holdin up with Mom? Don't let what she says bring ya down. I haven't even had time to think about Mom or Daddy.

I have to get some sleep. This heat never lets up man!

Sorry this is so long but I MISS you like cRaZy bro!

Your lonely sister lol, Erika

Then she noticed Billy had sent her a message.

Erika, glad you're having fun in China. We're okay here. John stayed over last night and we played some new games we found on the Web. So I'm cool.

I told ya China would be a stretch, but you just had to be with Monica J.

Love, your fave bro, Bill

The one from Grandma was too short.

Hi honey! Glad you made it to China and things are bearable. You'll get used to a lot of it and you'll miss it when you leave. I miss you! I'm leaving for a vacation in Minnesota for two months, remember? So I can't email you till you get home. Have a great time! It's the chance of a lifetime.

Love, Grandma

"Thanks for all the good information and comfort, you two." Erika snapped the laptop shut and stuck it in her bag. She knew what Billy would say if she confronted him: "I'm not much of a writer," or "I'm busy, too. I'll talk at you when you get home." Oh well, she'd survive. She'd already made up her mind about that.

In the bathroom her usual face looked back at her from the mirror. Somehow she expected to have grown Oriental features because she'd seen so many the past two days. The same nutmeg eyes under long golden lashes and a creamy complexion. Her seatmate on the plane from Chicago to Beijing said she sported a million freckles all jammed together. What was his name? Joseph. Long, lean Joseph, with blue eyes and golden hair. And no freckles. Lucky dude.

Half an hour later, Erika knocked on the door between her room and Monica's.

"Come in!"

She turned the knob and there stood Monica, beaming from across the room. "You look nice this morning."

"Thanks. You too."

Monica sported a red cotton skirt and t-shirt outfit. She tugged at the edge of Erika's red cotton t-shirt and glanced at her khaki walking shorts. "Designer shorts?"

"Wannabees." Erika put her arm around the older woman's shoulders. Monica responded with a hug around Erika's waist. "Mom doesn't have much money until Dad's life insurance is settled." She peeked at her tan leather sandals to make sure they were on straight.

"You should wear socks with your sandals. You

could get a disease from all the things you'll walk through."

Oh, yuck. Do I have to think about that stuff too? "Thanks. I'll think about it." *Nobody will ever, ever see me wearing socks with sandals. No way.* She changed the subject: "How about I fix your hair? I'll grab my gel."

"Sounds good." Monica stood in front of the mirror and watched Erika finger comb her hair. "I hope it lasts in this heat or a sudden rainstorm."

A couple of minutes later, Monica said, "Okay, let's go," and pulled her friend to the window. Together they leaned out from the third floor, on the back side of the Guesthouse, overlooking the street. The pair watched soldiers, business people and school children walking or riding bicycles and motorized rickshaws, cars and trucks below them. Monica chuckled as Erika mimicked the "beep-beep" from the bicycles and small cars.

The racket of hammers and saws drifted up from the construction sites. "Construction noise so early in the morning?" Erika turned to grab her bag and found her lip-gloss. She smeared the goop and rubbed her dry lips together as she returned to Monica's cozy shoulder hug.

"Owners switch crews morning and evening and work 24 hours a day." Monica raised the Bible she held in her left hand. "Let's share the Word like we did yesterday and pray before we start our day."

"Well, okay." Would she have to endure this prayer and Bible reading every day? She didn't mind when Monica did it, but she just didn't have the habit.

"How many verses have you memorized in Psalm 91?" Monica held her Bible as if it were her greatest treasure.

"Two."

"Okay. I'll listen, but you'll need to memorize a lot of verses."

"I worked on it last night, but I fell asleep."

"Yes, I saw your Bible on your bed."

"He that dwelleth in the secret place of the most High shall abide under the shadow of the Almighty. I will say of the Lord, He is my refuge and my fortress: My God, in him will I trust. Psalm 91:1, 2."

"Good job, Erika! I'm proud of you." Monica stuck her Bible into her backpack. "Let's pray." Monica bowed her head and Erika closed one eye. "Lord... ." Monica prayed, asking God's protection and care over them, the team and their families. "And help us remember why we're in China, to tell everyone we can about how much Jesus loves them. Amen."

"Amen." Erika glanced into Monica's dresser mirror. She tucked a loose wisp of hair into her braid and scooped her bag off the bed.

The two friends took the steps at a fast clip to the main floor. They zipped across the marble lobby and entered the dining room with Monica tipping her head slightly to everyone along the way.

"The food smells good." Erika sniffed. "I'd love a mocha latte." She noticed two older ladies pointing at Monica's feet and chattering.

Monica's eyebrows shot up. "What are they saying?"

— 7 —

WHERE'S THE LATTE?

Professor Bing rose from a nearby table and interpreted, "What are you doing wearing red shoes?" He bowed and Monica and Erika returned the gesture.

"Professor Bing, so good to see you! Do you always eat breakfast here?" Monica beamed at her supervisor.

"No, just when my wife visits her mother in Beijing." He started to sit back down, but the two older ladies pressed closer.

"I like red. It's my favorite color," Monica said to the two women, still chattering in Chinese.

"Oh, that is terrible, disgusting." Professor Bing fidgeted with his shirt collar as he interpreted. "I'm sorry, Monica," he said, "older people can be very direct."

Erika crossed her arms. Whew, they didn't give her the red hair and freckles routine she had learned to endure. She reached into her bag for her lip-gloss. *Monica says I have a nervous habit, applying lip-gloss all the time. Maybe I do*.

One lady pointed her walking cane at Monica. "How old are you?"

"I'm 68." Monica leaned forward slightly and smiled at the lady.

"You are wearing red shoes. That is not allowed in China."

"Why not?" Monica asked.

"You are too old to wear red shoes."

"They're very comfortable. Thank you for telling me." Monica glanced at her shoes, then back to the lady.

A white-haired woman touched Monica's blonde hair and then fingered her shirt.

"You asked me how old I am, how old are you?" Monica asked.

"I am 88."

Wow. *That lady's really pretty*, Erika thought. She pulled out her one-time use camera.

"You have lived a long time! What is your name?" Monica asked.

"Li."

"What is your family name?"

"Li."

Monica turned to the professor with a puzzled look. "What does this woman mean, Li Li?"

"At the time she was born, parents never gave girls a first name because they were not important." He coughed nervously and his eyes darted around the room. "Wives keep their own family name throughout their lives and the children take the father's name. When this woman was young, girls had no identity at all, just the family name, Li or Cao or whatever.

Monica's eyes filled with compassion and her voice sounded softer when she said, "You are so valuable to God." She waited for the interpretation. "You're special," she almost whispered.

Professor Bing cleared his throat and stumbled over the words. Erika realized he probably had never heard Monica's message before, either.

These people might as well get used to it, Erika thought. *Monica will say it a million times.*

Erika's stomach grumbled. She grabbed it as if to shut it up, smiling apologetically. Nobody seemed to notice.

The white-haired lady's expression remained blank. She brushed past Erika on her way to the front door.

"Do they say 'excuse me' in China?" Erika knew she could say it out loud because the women didn't understand English.

Monica's eyes followed the lady out the door. "She didn't understand what I was saying, and that is so sad." The Professor looked at Monica and blinked without saying anything.

Then the walking cane lady touched Monica's hair. *She's so short, she could walk under my arm if I held it out*, Erika thought.

Monica smiled at the tiny one. "Jesus loves you." She offered a hug but the lady pulled away, her eyes wide and her mouth in a large O. She twisted her hands together and said something.

"Ahh! This American foreign person is touching

me," Professor Bing interpreted with a chuckle.

"Erika, please take our picture." Monica stood close to the little lady, making sure she didn't touch her. "This is a good memory." Afterward, the woman scurried away with the expression of horror still on her face.

"She is not used to all the attention," the professor said.

Monica smiled. "Thank you for interpreting for us, Professor."

"I was glad to help." He glanced at Monica's Bible as he sat down in his place, but said nothing.

Monica and Erika scanned the dining room for their other team members.

"People are noticing your Bible," Erika whispered.

"Good." Monica and Erika both waved to the dining room hostess when they heard her say, "She's carrying a Bible."

"Hello, I am Luo Yang and I like your red shoes. Do not listen to those ladies." A tall man with a teapot on a long handle reached over a diner's shoulder and poured hot tea into his cup.

Monica and the tea server shook hands. "I always wear red. When I was seven years old, I saw a beautiful Chinese woman in a vision, wearing a red qi pao.[1] I didn't know then that I would ever visit China."

"Tell me the story." Luo Yang poured another cup of scalding hot tea.

[1]Sheepow, Chinese dress with a high Mandarin collar, cut in a straight line to the hem.

"We'll talk soon, but now we have to eat breakfast and go to our first class of the day." Monica and Luo Yang waved and Erika did too.

"I have heard about your classes. I may attend in the evenings," the tea server said.

"Great, we'll be glad to have you," Monica said and followed Erika between the tables.

"Good morning, nice to see you," Monica repeated over and over to the professors from the University and hotel guests in the dining room as she followed Erika past their tables.

"Good morning, Dr. Professor," they responded.

"How do they know you?" Erika scowled.

"Word gets around."

"And blonde hair sticks out in China." Erika tweaked a strand of Monica's hair.

"So does auburn hair." Monica flipped Erika's braid.

Erika said nothing.

Monica laid her hand on Erika's arm and made eye contact with diners who sat within close range, commenting, "This is Erika."

Erika tipped her head slightly and smiled as her name echoed across the tables. She couldn't make eye contact with all these people.

"There's the team." Erika led the way to their table. They joined four adults, Michael Dettmier, Robert Farnsworth, Daniel and Cheryl Carter, and their 16-year-old son Jesse.

"My classroom mates!" Twenty-year-old Michael stood up and hugged Monica first, then Erika.

"Good morning on our third day in this great land." Monica hugged everyone around the table, including the students who had come early to walk to class with the team.

"Hi, Miss Erika!" A young girl waved to her from behind Michael's chair.

"She remembered my name!" Erika waved back.

"Of course." Monica gave the girl a hug.

"But what is hers?" Erika rubbed her nose and scanned her brain pool.

"Carol, remember? Front row," Jesse commented over his bowl of rice.

"Yeah. Copies everything you say into her notebook." Erika sighed. Swarms of children meant swarms of names, too.

"Good morning!" Daniel stood up with the other team members to hug Monica and Erika. He had combed his short brown hair straight back, as usual, and his big blue eyes twinkled.

Daniel never loses his smile, ever, Erika thought. His comment from yesterday flashed through her mind. "I am ADHD and I have a lot of energy."

"Good morning!" Cheryl hugged Monica and Erika and sat down again. She leaned forward with her nose about four inches from the tablecloth, searching for something.

Cheryl's actions startled Erika because she had somehow forgotten that the lovely woman was legally blind. "Cheryl, you got me again. You seem to see everything like the rest of us."

"Lots of folks lose that mental note," Cheryl said as she pointed her eyes in the direction of Erika's voice.

"I'll put mine in a safe place this time." Erika plopped into the chair Michael held for her and Monica smiled at Jesse as he held her chair. Erika glanced up at the lights that were replicas of old lanterns around the walls. "Same beige walls, everywhere I go, but at least these lights are pretty."

Michael passed the bowls of food.

"Everything smells so good! I'm hungry! Rice and fish today, mmmm." Monica opened her napkin on her lap.

"I liked the noodles and shrimp we had yesterday." Cheryl skillfully manipulated her chopsticks.

Did she do that by the Braille method? *I'd have food all over the table if I couldn't see*, Erika thought.

Jesse sipped tea from his small cup. "I'm waiting for the morning we have eggs."

"I like eggs, too." Robert's six-foot body looked funny on the small dining chair.

Erika spooned some rice out of the bowl Jesse held for her. Yesterday Cheryl had said he was Korean and they adopted him when he was a baby. His even, white teeth showed in an ever-present smile.

"I'm dreaming of a mocha latte and a donut." Erika forked a bite of the rice and fish to her mouth. Oh, for just one little pancake with butter and syrup. Two months of rice and fish and rice and shrimp and rice and beans was a lot to bear, but she wouldn't think about it now. *I know*, she thought, *Monica says the Chinese are putting forth their best hospitality and we must show our appreciation.*

— 8 —

FIFTEEN STORIES UP

After breakfast, Erika sent Billy's email and carried her laptop upstairs to her room. She shouldered Monica's backpack and joined the team and a few students at the front door.

"Oh, by the way," Michael motioned for the team to come close. "Remember, we always need to help our students respect their teachers and we will put a *Mr*. or *Miss* with our name when we're around the students. And Monica wants to be called *Miss Wen Jing*."

"Okay, but we don't have to say it when we're away from the students, right?" Jesse twirled the backpack he carried.

"No, you can cut the titles when there aren't any students around."

Erika felt relief in her heart, but if things continued the way they had started, students would swarm around them most of the time.

Monica, Robert, Daniel and Cheryl set a fast pace on the one-mile walk to the English Building. Michael, nearly six feet tall with a high forehead and curly brown hair and brown eyes, joined Jesse and Erika. They pushed through the jostling carts, cars, bicycles and pedestrians. Erika's head buzzed at the constant beep beep and it jarred her nerves.

She stopped and tilted her head back to look up, up, up at the tall apartment buildings that rose from the sidewalk near them. "How many stories does that building have?" She pointed to her right.

"That one's 28 stories," Michael said, "but that one's 100 stories." He pointed to the left. Can you believe it? We climbed all the way to the top last summer because one of our students asked us to visit his apartment and meet his family. He lived on the 99th floor!"

"Do the elevators work in those buildings?" Erika couldn't stop staring.

"Not always on the first five-stories, but after that they usually have them. The one we visited had no elevator for a week. I guess we complained too much and the student told us when it started working again."

Michael stepped around a water buffalo tied to a coconut palm with a rope. "That seems like a small rope for such a big animal," he said. The animal kept on chomping the palm fronds that lay scattered under his feet.

Tantalizing aromas of spices and fresh produce drifted from the open market, along with revolting odors of cow dung and unwashed bodies. Flies buzzed everywhere, especially around the fresh meat lying uncovered in the bright sunlight. Erika started to gag at the sight of a headless goat, skinned and hanging on a nail that had been driven into a post.

Erika pointed to a house where the owners sold something white from a window. "What are those people selling?"

"Mantou bread." Michael wiped his perspiring face on his shirt tail. "It's just flour and water mixed up and fried on a griddle. I ate some last year and it's okay, kinda like our Ramen Noodles."

The team passed a huge wooden crate with chickens poking their heads out between the sticks that held it together. "Is that what live chickens smell like? Gross!" Erika held her nose.

"Yup. I remember that smell from last year." Michael held his forefinger horizontally under his nose.

"Oh, what cute little St. Bernard puppies." Erika stooped to pet a little head sticking out of the crate. "Do people have a lot of pets?"

"People buy them to eat." Michael poked his finger down his throat, pretending to gag. Jesse groaned.

Erika stopped, horrified. "That is disgusting! Will we have to eat puppies while we're here?"

"Maybe." Michael kept walking and Jesse and Erika trotted to catch up with him.

A lady carefully piled what looked like fresh eggs into a plastic bag. "They don't have egg cartons here?"

"No, she'll walk carefully all the way home." Erika laughed with the others as Jesse mimed a careful egg carrier.

Perspiration built damp splotches on everyone's clothing. The team members hugged the students they met along the way and gathered them into the group.

"How do they know us?" Erika shifted Monica's backpack on her shoulders.

"Word gets around, and besides, foreigners stick out among all these heads of black hair." Monica patted a boy's shoulder as they followed the sidewalk around a corner.

"Well, here we are." Michael dropped his backpack on the ground and bent his head back to look up at the 15 story English building.

"More students swarming around." Erika checked her reflection in the glass door. She straightened her top and patted her braid. Lipgloss? No time to apply it now. *I don't feel like being nice to all these kids today*, she thought.

"Do you remember your American name?" Michael asked the student who had stayed beside him all the way from the market. Erika wondered how the child had acquired his crooked nose and the scar over his right eye.

"Yes, I am Amos."

"I'm proud of you for remembering. What does *Amos* mean?"

"Kindhearted."

"Good name, and it seems to fit. Did you know there was an Amos in the Bible?"

"Maybe." Amos frowned and looked away.

Erika watched his eyes flicker like Billy's did when he fudged the truth a little. *He really doesn't know*, she thought.

Her eyes wandered to the huge resource book peeking out of the top of Monica's backpack. Cheryl had compiled one for each teacher, with Christian names and their meanings, games to play, idioms and other resources. Erika would have to carry the monster upstairs in the backpack, along with Monica's huge Bible and her bottle of water and other necessities.

"Good morning, Fred. So good to see you." Monica hugged the student. His ears looked fat, as if they were filled with polyester pillow stuffing.

"You remembered my name!"

"Of course."

"Is the elevator working this morning, Fred?" Monica pulled her own ears and finger combed her hair.

"I'll push the button." Fred used his thumb. The crowd watched for the light above the door.

"The light's not on." Several students, including Erika, scowled.

"The elevator repairman must still be on vacation and no one else can fix it. Up we go!" Monica led the way. "Climbing 15 flights of stairs will keep us in great shape. In 2004 we had only five flights and in 2005 we had 11."

Monica already dripped with sweat. *It has to be 120 degrees in this stairwell,* Erika thought.

Daniel and Cheryl followed Monica and the rest of the team and the students straggled behind them.

Erika wondered if anyone ever suffered heatstroke. *Dear Lord, don't let me be the first,* she prayed.

"I'm going to count the sweat drips on the stairs," she announced, but she stopped when Michael's big black tennis shoe obliterated at least twenty of them on the step in front of her.

A skinny girl with protruding teeth who looked about nine years old, followed close behind Cheryl. "Miss Cheryl, why do you always have your hand on Mr. Daniel's arm?"

"Miss Cheryl, this is Anna," Daniel said.

"Hello, Anna." Cheryl pointed her blue eyes in Anna's direction and smiled. "I don't see very well." Cheryl's short auburn hair glistened with perspiration and little drops clung to the ends. "I was born before I should have been, a premature baby. The doctors did wonderful things to help me live, but my eyes were damaged and I can't see more than two or three inches from my face."

"I will help, too." Anna looked into Miss Cheryl's eyes.

No one would ever know Cheryl couldn't actually see her. "Thank you." She smiled in Anna's direction. "You can help me find the bathroom when I need it."

Anna beamed as if Cheryl had asked her to become the queen of China.

Monica still led the way. "We figured it out this morning and climbing these stairs all summer will be like climbing the Great Wall 10 or 11 times."

Michael pointed to Monica. "You notice Monica isn't puffing?"

"You aren't puffing either, Michael."

"I'm glad I used a stepper machine at the club to get into shape. This heat and these stairs... ." Michael mopped his face with paper towels from the roll he carried, and offered them to the other climbers. The entire roll disappeared before the next landing.

Monica stopped on the 15th floor and the other climbers swarmed around her. "Michael, isn't it amazing that you, Erika and I were assigned the only air-conditioned classroom in the building? The rest of you are welcome to visit any time." She spread her hands and gave her best glowing smile.

Erika moved up beside Monica and the two of them looked over the rail at the students still climbing the steps. Jesse, Robert and the Carters opened their classrooms and turned on the ceiling fans.

Erika turned to open the door of their classroom but Monica didn't move. Instead, she raised her arms and whispered, "Thank you, Jesus, that we're here in this wonderful country among these precious people."

Erika rolled her eyes and wondered again what she was doing in this furnace called China. Feeling a little ashamed that she didn't share Monica's joy, she darted into their cool classroom, forgetting to close the door behind her. "Ahhhh." She spread her arms wide and inhaled the coolness. "Sorry," she whispered after someone slammed the door shut.

"Which classroom is yours?" the students asked among themselves. Yesterday Erika had helped assign them to the three different rooms, based on their age and English-speaking ability.

"We don't want to shame any student because she doesn't speak as well as the other students her age." Daniel's whispered words to Jesse had drifted to Erika as they ate breakfast. Jesse was a first tripper, too.

Thirty-five college age students and a few high schoolers crowded into the cooled classroom, chattering with excitement. Monica wiped her face with a paper towel as she watched them gather in the room.

— 9 —

MORNING CLASSES

Monica spread her arms wide and closed her eyes. "Jesus, please let the love I feel for these dear people show in my face." Three girls sitting on the front row pulled their eyebrows into deep-thought position and wrote something into their notebooks.

Erika guessed they were writing down Monica's prayer, whether they understood it or not. She applied lip-gloss. The girls around her eyed the little round jar but said nothing.

Then she realized her eyes were locked with those of a teenage girl across the room. They exchanged tiny waves. Erika searched her memory for the girl's name. *I helped her choose a name yesterday*, she thought. Oh, yes, *Amelia*, meaning industrious and independent.

Monica stood still again, arms outstretched, eyes closed. "This cool air feels so good. I'd forgotten how relentless the heat and humidity can be."

Erika thought of holding up her shirt just enough to let the coolness flow under it. Instead, she closed her eyes and concentrated on the coolness. When she opened them, four parents stood around her and Monica, grinning shyly.

Monica smiled into the parents' eyes. "Welcome." Everyone bowed. "Are you here for the classes?"

"Yes." A woman pointed to a teenager sitting at a desk. "My son Samuel." Erika had helped him decide between *Adam* and *Samuel* yesterday, and he'd chosen *Samuel*.

He stood up and bent his head slightly forward. "Our parents are in Mr. Daniel and Miss Cheryl's class, but they wanted to ask you a question."

"Okay, how can I help?"

"Why did you come here?" a mother asked and Samuel interpreted.

"In 1993 I picked up a card printed by the English as a Second Language China Group." Monica spoke slowly and waited for the children to interpret for their parents. "I read the question, 'Would you like to be a volunteer English teacher in China?'" I thought that would be a marvelous thing to do. I contacted the address on the card and they sent me an application. I filled out the application and in 1994 I made my first trip to teach at the Beijing College of Education. I have come almost every year since then."

By this time the entire class had gathered around to listen.

"Who sent you?"

"Jesus sent us."

"Who paid your way?"

"We always pay our own way."

"What? You paid to come here? Why?"

"Because we love you."

"How can you love us when you do not know us?"

"Jesus sent us. He loves you. He's the one who created you. He's the only true and living God."

Monica glanced at her watch and said, "It's time for class to begin. Please go to your own classrooms now. Erika kept her eyes fixed on Monica's face. She loved the way her smile radiated from her eyes. Why couldn't Erika smile the same way?

The parents left for the lower-skills classes, chattering in Chinese.

Monica's students headed for their seats with comments like, "Who is Jesus? Our teacher talks about him all the time." Then they sat quietly without talking because Chinese students are not allowed to talk much in school.

Erika waved to Amelia sitting in the second row. "Good morning, Amelia," she said at the same time Monica started talking.

Amelia nodded and smiled.

"Good morning, everyone!" Monica's smile made the room seem warm in a comfortable sort of way.

"Good morning, Miss Monica/Miss Wen Jing." The students giggled because some said one name and some said the other.

"Michael, Erika and I are glad to be here in Nanchong this morning." Monica slowly repeated the same thing she'd said the morning before.

The friendly lady should speak for herself, Erika thought. She itched to push a fast forward button as Monica droned slowly on. She had promised to talk faster next week after the students knew more English.

"Thank you for coming to our class. I know you have learned to *read* and *write* English in your schools, but the officials at the University have invited us to come and teach you to *speak* English."

"My American name is Monica Moore and my Chinese name is Wen Jing. Please call me Miss Wen Jing. Let's try it again. I will say 'good morning' and you will say, 'Good morning, Miss Wen Jing.'"

"Good morning."

"Good morning, Miss Wen Jing!"

Erika covered her mouth and struggled to fight back a smile because some of the students practically shouted their greetings.

"Very good!" The small woman pointed to the corner by the cooler where her young friend sat. "Now say good morning to Miss Erika."

"Good morning, Miss Erika."

Erika stood up, and smiled and waved. "Good morning, class." She still needed to get used to being called "Miss," but she felt more comfortable with the new title today. "I'm not missing anything," she'd wanted to yell at every student who called her "Miss Erika" yesterday.

"Now say good morning to Mr. Michael."

Everyone turned to look at the young man next to the door. "Good morning, Mr. Michael."

His dimple showed as he smiled and bowed.

"Good morning, class."

"Let's sing some songs and do the actions."

Monica started with,

"Heads and Shoulders, knees and toes,
Knees and toes, knees and toes,
Clap your hands and praise him."

The students jeered at one another, stretching and bending and trying to move their bodies as they sang the words. A teen named Peter lost his balance and fell headlong into the aisle. The whole class laughed and teased until Monica held up her hand. "We don't laugh at anyone who makes a mistake because Jesus would not laugh at him." Jeering faces turned somber in a heartbeat.

"Good job on the song." Monica and the students clapped. "That song worked out the sleepiness and you should be ready to sing some more." She led them in "Jesus Loves Me," "In Christ Alone I Stand," and "Nothing but The Blood of Jesus" while Erika pointed to each word on a chart-sized paper.

Erika flashed back to Monica's words before they left America, "Christian songs introduce the idea that Jesus loves them." Erika counted on her fingers. She and Billy had asked Jesus to be Lord of their lives six weeks ago! Monica's comments would have all been Greek to her then. Would Greek be worse than Chinese? There was no time to think about it.

"We have asked James to be our class monitor." Tall, thin James with a front tooth missing stood up beside his seat on the front row. His round face and full lips looked out of place on such a skinny body. "He will call the roll. Please say 'present' when you hear James call your American name."

A few forgot to say "present" when James called their names, but Monica did not allow anyone to jeer. "Jesus loves you just the way you are, and he would not laugh at your mistakes. We won't laugh, either."

Michael moved to the front of the room. "When I point to you, please stand up and tell us your name and its meaning. Then James will hand you a nametag. Please write your American name on it to help us remember."

Monica and Erika escaped to the hall while Michael supervised the roll call. They stepped aside for Anna, holding Cheryl's hand on the way to the bathroom.

"It feels like an oven out here." Erika waved her hand as a fan.

"Thank you, Lord, for our air-conditioned room," Monica said. They noticed Daniel next door wiping his perspiring face on his sleeve as he explained the daily proverb from the book of Proverbs. "The fear of the Lord is the beginning of wisdom," he said as he wrote the proverb on the board.

Monica and Erika bowed and smiled at the two Communist policemen standing rigid in the hallway, eyes straight ahead. "Good morning. Jesus loves you," Monica said with a warm smile. The policemen gave no response and a refreshing whoosh of cool air greeted the ladies as they stepped back inside the classroom.

"The Chinese are usually good students." Erika leaned down to hear Monica's whispered words. "They love to wear beautiful, neat clothes and receive attention from us because sometimes the teachers in the Chinese classrooms have 100 students in one class and they cannot give anyone special attention."

Erika gave a low whistle through her teeth. "And I thought American schools were overcrowded. Michael also said students go home exhausted because they work hard all day long on their studies."

"That's right. It's thrilling to see them relax and become talkative after they've been in our classes a week or two." Monica ran her fingers through her hair. "We give them a lot of personal attention and they begin to open up like little flowers."

Erika snapped her fingers on both hands at the same time. "I know! They're valuable because Jesus loves them."

Monica did a little jig right there. "Look how you've grown! A month ago you wouldn't have said that." The pair grabbed shoulders, touched foreheads and grinned. Monica dropped her arms and said, "We want to ignore their mistakes, knowing that they're going to beat themselves up any time they mess up."

"Not if you can help it, Miss Love Everybody." Erika slipped her arm around Monica's shoulders."

Monica hugged her back and started to the front of the room.

— 10 —

CLASSROOM CAPERS

Monica cleared her throat to get Michael's attention. "May I say something, please, Mr. Michael?"

"Certainly." He moved toward the back row.

"Students, you must open your mouth and speak out loud. Use your whole mouth to say each word." She exaggerated each syllable as she overstated her next sentence: "Don't keep your lips straight, don't say, 'mumble, mumble, mumble.'"

Everyone giggled.

"Thank you, Mr. Michael." Monica moved to the corner by the air-conditioner.

"You're welcome." Michael stood in the front and pointed to Carol in the first row.

She stood up and spoke loud and clear, "My name is Carol and it means 'Joy of God.'"

The two girls seated next to her stood up next.

"Marion means "'holy,'" the first girl said.

"Elizabeth means 'blessing.'" The third girl hid her face as if she felt shy.

Michael beamed. "Very good! I knew you could

do it."

Marion and Elizabeth grinned with pride and pleasure, but Carol's tiny smile barely lifted the corners of her mouth. Erika wondered if she could be intimidated around the older college students.

The class members shifted in their seats and grinned sheepishly when Monica said, "Now I want you to introduce your seatmate. Tell us his or her name and something about them. I'll go first and introduce Robert. Robert lives in America and he likes to chew bubblegum. Laugher. "Next." She pointed to a student in the front row.

He stood up and said, "This is my seatmate Joab and Joab is 16. He loves to play football. He likes to hide from his mother." Chuckles and clapping filled the room.

The remaining students introduced their seatmates until Monica said, "Everyone did great! I knew you could do it. Now you may ask a question and Mr. Michael or I will answer it. For example, 'What does a certain word mean?' Joab, what is your question?"

Joab stood up. "Mr. Michael, where do you live in America?"

"Good question, Joab." I live in Kearney, Nebraska." Michael pointed it out on the U.S. map. "Kearney is known for its university, called the University of Nebraska at Kearney."

Monica or Michael alternated answering the students' questions: "Do you get up early in the morning?"

"Do Chinese live in your town?"

"How many people live in your house?"

"What do you like best about China?"

Before the lunch break, Monica led the class in "The Hokey Pokey" until they collapsed in laughter on the floor.

I'm glad Billy can't see me now, Erika thought. *I'd never hear the end of it.*

Erika stood by Amelia and applied lip-gloss. She'd have to ask how to find the China University store and buy more.

Carol's hand went up in the front row and Michael nodded in her direction. "May we sing 'In Christ Alone I Stand ' again?

"Certainly." Monica motioned for Erika to find the chart with the words and hold it up. Carol sang loud and clear all the way through. *Monica said the students hear the entire gospel story in that song*, she thought.

Erika wondered if Carol and her friends would always sit in the front row and copy everything Monica wrote on the board. Good night, carrying those notebooks for two months would develop huge muscles on the girls' skinny bodies. She couldn't stifle a snicker at the thought of Carol with a bodybuilder's muscles.

Billy would rebel at repeating whatever the teacher said out loud, over and over, memorizing everything. Or copying everything into a notebook. Erika blocked the tears of homesickness before they started and decided it was time for more lip-gloss and a drink of water.

Monica glanced at her watch and said, "Class is

dismissed for lunch. Bring something for show-and-tell tomorrow, something you can tell the class about. Pictures of family, things that are special to you."

As Monica helped Erika put away the song charts, she said, "We'll have show-and-tell often because the students get to stand up in front of a group and begin to feel more confident. They love it." Monica hugged any students who passed her on their way out the door.

"They like your hugs, just like I do," Erika said. She hugged Monica and received a gentle bear hug and a kiss on the cheek in return. The teen embraced one young girl who reached out to her.

"That's nice." Monica smiled and patted Erika's arm.

Everyone bowed to the Communist policemen in the hall, but the men stood stock still and expressionless, as usual.

Amelia watched while Erika and Monica slipped her two-month planner into her backpack. Then the two teens inspected a U.S map from the American Automobile Association, *AAA in my mind*, Erika thought.

Monica joined them and said, "I give a puzzle to the student who recites the most state capital names from memory."

"Then I'd better start memorizing," Amelia said as she folded the map and returned it to the backpack.

"Good. It would be a privilege to give you a puzzle." Monica patted Amelia's arm.

Also in the backpack was a folder on various ways to stimulate conversation and speak, and skills every person should use, such as introducing one another, saying "thank you," and "please" and showing appreciation.

Monica said, "I'll assign essays, too, and require the students to read them in front of the class."

"I like to write essays," Amelia said.

"Most Americans could use this one," Erika muttered under her breath and glanced at the information and games Monica had brought along for teaching telephone etiquette and proper ways to interact with adults.

"Most Chinese need it too," Amelia said, and both girls chuckled. "Democracy?" the beautiful Chinese teenager asked as she read the label on the folder in a section marked "Cultural Lectures."

"Yes," Monica said, "ideas such as holding elections in the class, campaigns and speeches and running for office fit well with teaching The Ten Commandments as the basis for Western law. We introduce Jesus as the only one who makes it possible to fulfill the principles God wrote in the Commandments."

Amelia turned as two other students motioned for her to join them. "We all live in the same apartment building. See ya."

"See ya." Erika picked up Monica's backpack and headed down the steps with the "Cool Team." Jesse had nicknamed them that, "Because your room is cool, get it?"

Erika got it and thanked God again for the cooler, and for Jesse on the team.

Her friend and mentor never missed a chance to teach her team. As they descended the steps, Monica said, "I affirm the students, I tell them, 'I like the way you speak English.' We teach our students to look people in the eye as though they really respect them and value their friendship. We don't allow them to mumble and look away."

"Just like you taught me." Erika stopped a moment to stuff her straw bag into the backpack.

"Yes, you were a wonderful student."

Erika grinned and crossed her arms. "But there are so many people in China, I feel like they're swarming all over me."

"Just keep trying to look people in the eye." Michael playfully tapped her on the head with his umbrella.

The threesome bowed to two policemen on the tenth floor landing and Monica kept on, "We teach them a lot of etiquette, like how to shake hands properly, not like a wet noodle, and say, "I'm glad you're here in my country. I'm really glad to know you."

She'd said it all before, but Erika wouldn't remind her.

Michael's heavy shoes thumped on the steps. "Someday we'll have to count the steps." He stopped to tie his shoestrings.

"Or count the steps on one flight and multiply that number times 15 flights." Then Erika had a thought and laughed out loud. "If we were in a cartoon strip, my feet could be as big as yours, Michael," she said.

"What brought that on?" Michael obviously didn't appreciate her joke.

Oooops! Time to change the subject.

"One more time down the mountain." Erika paused at the last landing. "One, two, three... ."

"Oh, here's the rest of our team," Monica said and patted Cheryl's shoulder.

"... fourteen, fifteen, sixteen. Let's see, what is 16 steps multiplied by 15?" Erika counted on her fingers. "Two hundred forty. Did you know we climb 240 steps to our classrooms?"

"Oh, yeah! That's cool, Team." Jesse grinned and faked a basketball shot.

— 11 —

LUNCH

"Ready?" Daniel set a fast pace back to the Guesthouse with Cheryl, Robert and Monica. Erika, Michael and Jesse checked out the places of interest on the busy sidewalk.

"Amelia invited me to come to her apartment tomorrow," Erika said as she flicked a fly off her arm and cringed at sight of the hideous, crawly thing.

"Great, it'll be good for you to have a Chinese friend." Michael swatted a mosquito on his arm. "Oh, oh, it looks like I need more bug spray from the CU store."

"Monica and I take Vitamin B pills to keep them away. And we use bug spray too," Erika said.

"Let's go to the campus store after Cultural Lectures this afternoon. Jesse, you too?"

"Okay." Jesse stooped to pet a furry animal jammed into a crate at the market.

"That thing looks a lot like a cat but it has more teeth than my neighbor's cat back home," Erika said. "What is it?"

"A civet cat." Jesse jumped back when it hissed at him. "You'll get inside a real Chinese home, Erika, if you make friends with Amelia."

"Yeah." Erika held her nose. "Those civet cats stink."

"They're pretty dirty," Michael said, "and they have a scent gland like a skunk. It smells like the whole crateful has been using theirs."

"Eeew! And people eat these?" Erika took a step backward, away from the crate.

"Yeah, they do... ." Jesse glanced at the sky. "It sure looks cloudy."

Michael wrinkled his nose. "Sheesh, those aren't clouds. That's pollution making the sky gray. Sick."

"The sun is just a ball of orange in the middle of the day." Jesse shoved his shades on top of his head and his ears stuck out because the bows pushed on them.

"The big cities like Nanchong and Shanghai have a problem with pollution." Michael pulled his camera out of his backpack. Some students straggled past as he clicked photos.

The threesome caught up with the older adults as Jesse said, "The air smells funny. Will it be different inside the Guesthouse?" He did a bunny nose twitch and Erika snickered.

"Not without air conditioning and the windows all open." Cheryl sneezed as they entered the hotel lobby. "I can't wait to change out of these wet clothes."

Monica touched her own perspiration-soaked

shirt. "What a blessing that Gloria made arrangements for someone to wash all of our clothes."

"Yes, Gloria and the other CU staff members are a real blessing." Cheryl still held Daniel's hand.

"But especially Gloria." Daniel glanced at the students and other people around them. "Lots of listening ears here." *He didn't mention that Gloria and her husband Ralph are secret believers because they could be imprisoned and persecuted if the Communist officials find out*.

Erika flashed back to the way Monica talked about Jesus and used the Bible in the classes. Monica had said Americans will be sent home if the Communist officials decide to stop them from evangelizing, but the Chinese are imprisoned and persecuted. Erika tried to make sense of it all.

Everyone on the team knew Gloria. She had repented of running her own life in 1996 after Monica shared *Step Up to Life* and studied the Bible with her at China University in Beijing. Gloria told her husband Ralph about her decision and he asked to pray with Monica too.

Gloria moved from China to Seneca in 2000 while she studied for her masters in business administration at the University of Kansas. Three years later, the entire family moved to Seneca while Ralph earned his masters degree in education.

"Meet you in the dining room after we all shower." Daniel still held Cheryl's hand as they climbed the steps to their room.

"See ya." Robert disappeared to his own room on the second floor.

"It'll take five." Jesse scoped the steps two at a time, to the second door past his parents' room on the third floor.

"I'm already there." Michael headed for the door next to Jesse's.

*   *   *

Monica and Erika had barely found a table in the dining room when Daniel and Cheryl arrived for lunch. "Oh, this looks good! Smells good too!" Daniel seated Cheryl and sat down. The team hugged a few students standing around the table. Erika cringed at the thought of making contact with those sweaty little bodies, but she hugged the children anyway. Monica would want her to.

Steamy bowls of rice, soup, corn kernels, eggplant, chicken, tofu and orange fish gave off tantalizing smells from the large turning tray on their table.

"I wish we could eat one meal in peace without all these kids around," Erika grumbled. "I dreamed about them last night, only they turned to ants, crawling all over me."

Michael squeezed Erika's shoulder but said nothing. She cringed inside at the sight of food. Monica had said she must eat and keep up her strength. Would three spoonfuls do?

"Chopsticks anyone?" Daniel reached for his own set by his plate and handed Cheryl's to her.

"I've been to China ten times already and I like to use them." Monica expertly tasted the tofu. "Robert and Michael, you like them, too?"

Two nodding heads confirmed Monica's words because their mouths were too full to speak.

Jesse stared at Monica as she skillfully lifted a bite of watermelon to her mouth. He picked up his own chopsticks.

"I will help you." A student stepped up to the table and Jesse checked the kid's nametag.

"Yes, Peter, please show me."

Peter shoved his glasses up on his nose.

"Me too." Erika picked up her chopsticks. *Chopsticks, snopsticks. What difference does it make? I'd better go along with this*.

Peter demonstrated: "Hold one chopstick between your pinky finger and ring finger. You will keep it still and not move it. Hold the other chopstick above it, between tall finger and pointer finger. You will manipulate this chopstick to pick up the food. Like this."

Other diners laughed at the clumsy Americans. Erika stuck a chopstick in her braid, mimicking Dr. Du's ivory one. Jesse held one between his teeth and growled fiercely. Michael tried to lift a piece of fish, but it plopped onto the floor and rolled underneath the table. He crawled under the table after it and bumped his head. "Ouch!"

Erika laughed out loud and managed to lift something with her chopsticks. "What's this?"

"Eggplant." Monica drank soup from her bowl and wiped her mouth on her napkin.

"Wait till I tell Billy I ate eggplant. . ." A minute later she said, "Well, it's no mocha Frappaccino, but at least I'm not gagging."

Carol and her friends grinned at the messy Americans, spilling food onto the table and floor. Monica hugged them. "Welcome. I appreciate the way your group always comes to class early and copies everything from the board."

The four friends smiled and linked arms.

Monica cupped Carol's chin in her hand. "You're 13 years old?"

"Yes, Miss Wen Jing." Carol tipped her head slightly.

"How old are you, Elizabeth?" Michael asked. He must have remembered her name from class.

Erika accidentally slurped her soup. "Excuse me."

"In China it's okay to slurp." Jesse grinned over the rim of his bowl.

"I am 14." Elizabeth pointed to the others. "Joseph is 12. Marion is 13."

"We were hoping for an English teacher to come help us have some experience speaking." Carol laughed again at the Americans' antics.

"You all do very, very well with your English," Monica said and reached for more rice. "That's why you're in the college-age class. Jesus said, 'I will make a way for you,' and he made a way for you to speak English correctly."

Erika noted the questions in their eyes at the mention of Jesus' name.

Monica must have noticed too because she said, "I will tell you more about Jesus."

"I want to hear more." Joseph leaned on Jesse's chair.

"They're very sure of themselves," Cheryl said, smiling and holding her bowl and chopsticks close to her face. She knocked her glass of water over without realizing it, and Jesse tossed a wad of napkins onto the puddle. He didn't say anything, probably because he didn't want her to feel clumsy.

Erika overheard Michael mumbling to Daniel when she turned to watch him use his chopsticks: "I'm trying to be intentional about looking them in the eyes, making sure each one feels welcome every single day." He expertly lifted a piece of chicken to his mouth. Erika tried it too.

"I did it!"

"Good job, Erika!" Robert's grin said it all.

"So much of our evangelism is through loving them, not through preaching at them," Daniel mumbled back to Michael. "Their teachers and family never tell them they are loved and suddenly they have to understand an abstract God they can't see, who loves them."

Michael waved as the students left for home and said, "We really love you guys, and Jesus loves you. See ya around 2:30 when we walk back to Cultural Lectures."

The children waved on their way out the door of the Guesthouse.

I hope they start playing computer games at home and forget to come back, she thought. Sometimes all those kids felt like the swarms of ants on that anthill she'd accidentally stood on in eighth grade summer camp. At least these kids didn't bite her ankles.

She could never tell Monica how irritated she felt when they gathered around her and insisted on touching her hair or rearranging her braid. Next thing they would ask to undo the braid and make her sit down so they could comb it and re-style it. *How can I learn to like these kids instead of detesting their attention?*

— 12 —

CULTURAL LECTURES

The team climbed the Guesthouse stairs after lunch and headed to their own rooms.

"Monica, I'm gonna go write Billy an email unless you need help with something." Erika applied lip-gloss.

"That's fine. Just be sure to take a little nap. It will help in this heat." Monica opened the door between their rooms for more air circulation as Erika unlatched her laptop cover.

> *Hey Bro, thanx for the little note yesterday. It seems like I'm writing you all the time. Only I wish you'd write me a little more :P. I really miss ya Bro. Tell me everything I've missed. Catch me up man.*
>
> *I feel mega better today. It helps a ton to have a friend my age too. Amelia is sixteen like us. She's in Monica's and Michael's and my class because she speaks English so amazingly well. She's a freaking genius man! Otherwise she wouldn't be in the college age*

class. I'm hanging out with Jesse and Michael too, they are a blast!

The kids seem to like bein around me, especially if I let them play with my hair. I joke around a lot with the teenagers and college kids.

It's still bizarre here! And being with Monica is still the only reason I can stand it. I think I help her a lot? Like last night I ran up to her room and got her camera so she didn't have to. I also help her lots in the classroom.

She helps me tons too. Last night I woke up screaming cuz I dreamt Mom beat me up and shoved me into the closet like she normally does ya know?

Monica came running in. Lots of tears and kleenexes and me hiccupping really loud came next. But she rubbed my back like Daddy used to, remember? Then she just held me and hummed "Amazing Grace". When I calmed down, she looked me in the eyes and said, "I love you, Erika." The tears and hiccups started all over again. And she held me again.

I told her I miss Daddy so much! And when she asked why I woke up screaming I told her about my dream. She kinda shuddered. Then she prayed and asked God to comfort me and held me tighter.

She said I have to forgive Mom. I couldn't even talk for a long time, with all the horror in my head, but I finally said I couldn't forgive her. Monica said all God requires is that I want to forgive Mom and he'll take care of the rest.

She asked if she could coach me in a prayer. She prayed something about me wanting to forgive Mom, and asking God to help me, and I said it after her. I didn't really want to, but I prayed the prayer for Monica. She rubbed my back til I fell asleep.

Amelia asked me to go to her apartment with her tomorrow. Monica's glad I get to visit a real Chinese home. I really like Amelia. She's beautiful. She's got short hair, and it's black of course. She's about my height with a dark brown mole like a star on her upper lip. Monica calls it a turkey bite cuz she said it's sorta like a turkey bit her and left a mark.

I really miss Seneca a lot, and my cell phone, and my MP3 player, and hamburgers, and fries, and basically normal food. But not nearly as much as my favorite brother J.

Write! Write! Write!

Love ya lots, Bro.

Erika the beautiful :P

The team met in the lobby around 2:30 p.m. "Everybody got your hand fan and your Bible? And your umbrella in case it rains?" Michael waggled the items in his hands.

"Sure do."

"Yes, one fan for each hand, and an umbrella."

"Got 'em."

"All safe from my sweat in this plastic bag."

"I brought these extras for the students who don't have any." Robert held up a box of fans.

"Cultural lectures, here we come." Erika applied lip-gloss and ran to meet Amelia who wore a peach silk flower in her hair and orange shorts. Her white t-shirt with peach trim already showed splotches of perspiration. The girls whispered and giggled next to Jesse and Michael as they walked through the crowds and past the market.

"What do we do in the Cultural Lectures?" Amos asked. "I had to watch my little cousin yesterday. I could not come."

"Everyone is welcome to come in the afternoon," Michael said. "We discuss the United States, its regions, our holidays, our government, our history, business, economics, cultural things."

"The Chinese are sharp mentally, and very, very precious." Cheryl's hand rested on Daniel's arm. "You have to keep up with them and try to stay ahead of them, if you can."

"Remember, our goal is to get them to speak English." Monica's eyes twinkled. "If we have the students speaking English and everyone participating, the officials will overlook the fact that we're talking about Jesus."

"Monica is very, very bold," Daniel spoke directly to Jesse. "It's such a joy to come to China with her. While we're here each year, by loving each person individually, the love of Christ comes through. I'm always astounded at the percentage of students who make Jesus Lord of their lives."

"I've had contact with a lot of them through e-mail," Robert chimed in, "and they almost always remain faithful to the Lord. They know that becoming a Christian in China could cost them their jobs, their freedom, and their safety. They become special targets of the police and they're beaten and put in jail."

"Last year I realized that being with Monica is like walking with a modern-day Moses," Michael said, "because it seems like the sea just parts and we walk right through. It's an exciting experience."

Erika noticed the tiny smile that lifted the corners of Monica's mouth. "It's all the prayers of the people back home that make it possible to do what we do," she said.

Michael waved to a little boy watching them from an apartment window.

Jesse held the door at the English building. The crowd scrambled inside to escape the sudden heavy rain shower.

"I didn't know that was coming." Jesse used his shirttail to wipe the rainwater off his arms.

"It comes fast every time, but it doesn't last long," Michael said, wiping his arms too.

Erika grinned. She'd made it inside before the rain caught the others.

"We have twice as many students this afternoon as we had this morning." Daniel started cleaning the raindrops off his glasses as he trudged up the steps. "I haven't seen most of these people before. Word must have really gotten around from yesterday."

Erika started up the stairs, cringing at the odor of wet clothing on all the little bodies. She totally forgot to reply to Daniel.

She noticed Fred, Amos and Joab helping a boy, about 10 years old in a wheelchair. *Unbelievable! They're going to carry that kid up all these steps in that wheelchair!* She grinned at the boy and said, "What's your name?"

"Abraham." The boy clung to the arms of the wheelchair as if he thought the boys might drop him.

"Where did you get that name?" Erika asked.

"Joab and Fred gave it to me. Fred almost picked it for himself." He obviously didn't have time for talking because he concentrated so hard on his bumpy ride.

"Welcome to Cultural Lectures. We're glad you're here." Erika climbed past them a step or two and caught up with Amelia. She could still hear the boys grunting and straining as they struggled with the heavy wheelchair.

"Can we help you?" Erika turned when she heard two college age men come up behind the three boys and the wheelchair.

"No thank you. We can do it," Joab said and pushed hard on the chair.

On the third flight of stairs she heard a loud voice, "Amos, hold up your end. We cannot hold him alone." She whirled in their direction and horror filled her heart.

Amos must have stumbled and dropped his corner. "Watch out!" Fred yelled. "He is going to fall!"

The wheelchair teetered on the stair, leaned too far back and plunged backward down ten steps. Chaos broke out with screaming students flying everywhere behind the wheelchair, all the way to the landing.

Abraham screamed too but fell silent as he landed, half in and half out of the chair, then toppled out of it. Erika's stomach wrenched and terror filled her heart as he lay still with his neck at an odd angle on the first step.

"God help us!" Monica and Michael said together as they plowed through the path the students made for them from the head of the line. Daniel and Cheryl followed and all four team members formed a tight circle, praying softly and trying to shield Abraham from the terror-filled eyes of the students.

"Let's pray," Monica commanded calmly. "God can heal this boy. What is his name?"

"Abraham," Erika replied from behind her.

"Abraham, a man in the Bible who had great faith," Michael said and placed his hand on Abraham's head. Daniel touched his shoulder and Cheryl wrapped her arms around Amos, Fred and Joab who stood sobbing behind Daniel.

Monica laid her hand on Abraham's crooked neck and Erika felt her own faith rise. *God can heal him. I believe he will*, she thought and stretched her own hand in Abraham's direction. Jesse and Amelia came up beside her on the third step.

"Father, we know that if two or more people agree on anything in prayer, it will be done," Monica prayed. "We believe it is your will to heal Abraham. In the name of Jesus, we command him to be healed. Abraham, in the name of Jesus, rise up and walk. 'Whatsoever you shall pray in faith believing shall be done,'" she quoted from the Bible and continued praying quietly. Those who had been touching Abraham removed their hands from his body. Everyone on the team bowed their heads and prayed. Some of the students, especially the high school and college agers, joined in.

Abraham's eyes fluttered open. He looked around at the people he could see from where he lay. He moved his head and his neck cracked. Loud. It cracked again and a huge smile spread across his face. Monica took his hand and helped him sit up.

"His neck! It's straight!" A babble of voices rose in the stairwell along with sobs and shouts. "Jesus healed him."

A short, skinny, fidgety man blinked from the top step of the second flight of stairs and said nothing. Erika noted the moles on the end of his nose and eyelid and wondered why he was so interested in Abraham's healing. Could he be a government spy?

Amid the chaos, Abraham held tight to Monica and Michael's hands and pulled his legs under him.

"He's standing up! He couldn't walk before!" The students began clapping and cheering. "Stand up, Abraham! Stand up!" Erika's ears rang from the deafening roar but she didn't care.

Abraham grinned at his cheering coaches and took a tiny step toward Monica. His Jack o' Lantern smile matched hers. Michael held him, careful to allow space for walking.

Slowly Abraham released Monica and Michael's hands and walked across the landing. Three students Erika didn't know snatched the wheelchair away. People standing on the first and second flights of steps passed it down to the door.

The clapping and cheering continued and Abraham grinned as he followed Monica and Michael through the path to the head of the group. Daniel and Cheryl grabbed hands with Amos, Joab and Fred and the five of them moved to the head of the line too.

The climbers surrounded Abraham as they reached the top landing, crowding against the two policemen, clapping and cheering. Abraham said, "God healed me!" over and over and kept his huge smile going until Michael rescued him and escorted him into the cool classroom.

Someone had gone to fetch Abraham's parents. They came huffing and puffing up the stairs, grinning and hugging their son, speaking in Chinese and listening as other students seemed to explain what had happened. Erika invited them into the classroom when it became obvious that they were not about to let go of Abraham for a minute.

Monica and the team greeted them with hugs and smiles. A student who looked like a college professor seemed to explain the events over and over in Chinese until the parents relaxed. They finally sat down in the chairs Michael and Jesse found for them.

The cloudburst failed to cool the building and the 104 degree heat seared through the outside walls. Erika and Amelia tried to keep Monica's classroom door closed while the rest of the team found seats for nearly 100 people on the floor, around the walls or on whatever chairs they could find.

"I'm glad my classroom is nice and big," Monica said, "and we can meet in this cool room."

Daniel and a college student held their shirt collars out near the air conditioning unit. "This feels so good, but that small floor unit isn't made to keep 100 people cool."

Erika and Amelia sat cross-legged near the unit. "What is that?" Amelia asked, looking curiously at Erika's small jar, and Erika wondered what took her so long to ask.

"It's lip-gloss to keep your lips moist. Smell it." Erika held it out.

Amelia sniffed. "Ummm. Strawberry."

"We'll get you some at the CU store this afternoon," Erika said. "Want to come with us? Michael, Jesse and I are going right after Cultural Lectures."

"Yes, I'd love to." Amelia screwed on the lid and handed the jar back as Monica stepped to the front. All talking stopped.

"Let's pray." Monica walked across the small area set aside for the classroom stage and touched the short, fidgety man's shoulder. His moles stood out on his pale face and he refused to look up at her. Erika guessed that the team leaders had figured out he was a government spy. *He's so nervous,* she thought.

"Please bow your heads and close your eyes." Monica thanked the one living God for the opportunity these precious Chinese people had to learn oral English. "If the Son (Jesus) shall make you free, you shall be free indeed," she quoted from the Bible.

Erika noticed Spy Man glance at the door and half rise from his seat when Monica finished her prayer. Then he sat back down and took out a notebook. *Spies always take notes*, she thought.

"Monica and the leaders know who the government spies are, but they don't care," Erika whispered to Jesse.

Jesse's perfect teeth flashed. "Yeah, I know. They still want everyone to hear about Jesus even if the government sends us all back home early."

"Wow! Why did I tell you something you already know? I'm such a dork!"

— 13 —

CROWD IN, EVERYONE!

"Good thing we have these hand fans." Erika waved hers at Amelia who waved back, fast, in a contest, until Amelia's broke. "Oh, sorry." Erika got Amelia a new one from Robert's box.

"All your waving sorta cooled me off," Jesse said. "It's getting hot in here."

"Monica doesn't even notice the heat. She's so sweet to everyone," Erika said, nodding her head in rhythm to the CD that played across the room. When "In Christ Alone I Stand" began playing, everyone from the morning classes sang along.

"Hi, Professor Bing!" Erika waved to him as he squeezed into a small space by the door. There was no room to stand up, but he smiled and bowed his head slightly.

"Professor Bing! I'm so glad you came this afternoon!" He gave a slight nod and a smile to Monica as she gave him her special huge smile.

"She's crazy about these people," Erika whispered to Jesse. "but honestly... . Erika stopped mid-sentence. I was going to say I want to go home, but

I realize I'm not that homesick any more. I'm glad I came with Monica." He gave her a high five, but didn't reply.

Erika jumped up from her floor seat when Monica handed her a chart to hold up.

"Who can tell me what an idiom is?" Monica looked around. Snickers and whispers filled the room. Finally a man about thirty with glasses and thinning hair in front stood up and said, "An idiom doesn't fit the rules of the language, but everyone knows the meaning. 'Back seat driver' refers to the habit a person has of telling the driver how to handle a car. Sometimes it means a person is giving too much unwanted advice."

"Very good, and what is your name?"

"I am Wang Jinrong, but I prefer to be called Martin. I am a professor here at the University."

"Thank you for your help, Martin. Welcome to Cultural Lectures." Martin bowed and sat down.

Erika flipped the charts and Monica read off four more idioms with explanations for each one.

"Thank you, Erika. I appreciate your help." Monica smiled as Erika plopped down next to Amelia. "Let's clap to show how much we appreciate her."

Erika's face felt hot but she managed to smile and wave anyway.

Michael took center stage as the clapping wound down. "What is a holiday?" he asked.

Martin was the only one who held up his hand. "A day when everyone stays home from work and celebrates a special occasion."

"Very good, Martin." Michael fanned himself vigorously. Thanksgiving is one of the major American holidays." He handed Erika a picture of a turkey to hold up. "I know you don't have turkeys in China. This is a male turkey, a gobbler."

"Gobbler, gobbler, gobbler" echoed over the room as students practiced saying it, and poked each other. Michael briefly told the story of how the Indians helped the Pilgrims survive in 1620. He explained the settlers' faith in an invisible God who sent the Indians to help them. Erika, Amelia and Jesse passed out candy corn as reminders of the corn the Indians helped the Pilgrims plant. The students giggled and popped the orange and yellow goodies into their mouths.

"What is the meaning of *thanksgiving*?" Michael asked.

Carol raised her hand. Michael nodded and she said, "Thanksgiving is when we appreciate something and say thank you to the person who gave it to us."

"Very good, Carol." Then Michael asked, "How can we show that we are grateful to God for everything he provides?"

The students exchanged glances but no one responded. Slowly Erika's hand went up.

"Yes, Erika," Michael said with a smile.

"We can tell others what God has done for us, and sing about him in songs." Erika smiled because she suddenly felt happy inside.

"Good job, Erika!" Monica's grin showed how pleased she was that Erika responded so well.

"By the way," Michael interrupted himself, "we're showing a film Saturday afternoon at three, and you're all welcome to come. The film is called *Jesus* and it will answer many of your questions about him."

"Watch Spy Man squirm," Erika whispered to Jesse.

"Yeah. Our teaching contract doesn't say we have to have classes afternoons, evenings and weekends, but the spies come anyway." Jesse popped another handful of candy corn into his mouth.

Michael motioned to her and Erika held up pictures of traditional Thanksgiving foods. He explained the symbolism for each item, especially turkey, cranberries and pumpkin pie. Amelia and Jesse passed out dried cranberries. Again, smiles all around.

"Do you have any questions?" Michael and Monica surveyed the crowd.

Carol stood up. "I thought people gave thanks to the Indians on Thanksgiving Day."

Monica put her hand on Carol's shoulder. "That's true, but the Pilgrims wanted to thank God for helping them survive the cold winter, grow good crops and build warm houses."

"I didn't know that!" Carol's eyes grew wide.

People in the class looked surprised. "I didn't know that" came from all directions. Spy Man still squirmed.

"She has said a thousand times that God covers her and she can safely say all those things about Jesus," Erika whispered to Jesse.

"She also says she counts on the prayers from home," he whispered back, and Erika grinned.

Then Michael and the teens tacked a cartoon donkey, minus its tail, on the bulletin board at the front of the room.

Monica held up the donkey's tail and a jar of pencils. "The one who pins this tail closest to the right place will receive one of these red, white and blue pencils."

"Oooohhh! I want one of those," rippled across the room.

Erika wanted one too. She caught her friend's eye and pointed to herself so that Monica would know, and they grinned.

"Who's first?" Michael held up the donkey tail with a thumbtack in the top. Erika heard a commotion and realized the students were shoving Abraham onto the stage area. She tied on the blindfold as he came to stand in front of her and turned him around several times. He swayed a little and then walked straight across the little stage area and poked the tack with the tail into the bulletin board. His big grin under the lopsided blindfold looked ridiculous, but the class had learned not to poke fun at anyone. They did laugh with him when he pulled off the blindfold and discovered he'd pinned the tail two feet from the donkey!

Erika noticed Abraham's parents in the second row. They could not take their eyes off their son. *He's such a handsome kid, but it didn't show in that wheelchair*, she thought.

"Nice try, Abraham." Michael marked his place with a huge blue tack, took the blindfold and tied it on Amelia. She and two other students from the morning classes took turns. Amelia's tack came closest and she danced a little jig when Michael handed her a prize pencil.

"That looks like fun. I would like to try." Professor Bing pushed his way through the students on the floor and raised his hands in a victory sign as the class cheered. Erika knotted the blindfold and turned him around and around.

"Where is that donkey?" Professor Bing turned to the right, then to the left, and walked straight toward Fred and Amos on the floor. They clapped their hands over their mouths and scooted away from him, but he kept walking, slowly, with the tack sticking straight out, ready for a big push into the bulletin board.

"There!" Professor Bing pushed the tack in the air.

"Ow, ow, ow, I did not think you would push so fast!"

"Oh, no!" Professor Bing yanked down the blindfold. He'd shoved the tack into Fred's nose! "Oh, oh, I am so sorry!" Laughter exploded in the room and Professor Bing hurried to his seat, head down.

"Let's clap for Professor Bing," Michael said and started clapping. Erika applauded harder than anyone. When he saw her, Professor Bing raised his head and grinned. Erika thought she felt the classroom rock with the applause.

Michael and Monica examined Fred's nose. "It's just a scratch. He'll be okay," Monica said and applied a band-aid from her first aid kit.

Michael divided the group into three teams by counting off and saying "one," "two," or "three" when their turn came. Each group chose a classroom and spent the next half hour doing The Hokey Pokey and other dances the morning students had learned.

At five, every student left the classroom. Erika loaded the files and classroom materials back into Monica's backpack. "Monica, I need to buy more lip-gloss at the CU store. I have enough money to buy some for Amelia. She's going with me too."

Monica handed her the backpack. "Okay, but who else is going with you?" Whew! Monica sure was a nag about the team rule, "Don't go anywhere alone."

"Jesse and I need to buy bug repellant and we'll all walk together." Michael's brown eyes twinkled. "Cultural lectures were fun today, huh?"

"Yes. Our spy was nervous after I prayed for him. Did you get his name?"

"No, and he may not give it to us unless he has to." Michael held the door for the Cool Team.

Monica headed toward the stairs with Daniel, Cheryl and Robert, but she stopped suddenly when she spied Martin standing in the hall. "You're still here!"

— 14 —

MARTIN

"I've been waiting to talk to you," Martin said as he and Monica shook hands.

Erika glanced back at them from the stairs and called, "Michael, Jesse, Amelia and I are headed for the campus store," but Monica was busy talking to Martin and didn't reply.

Jesse jumped up and touched the ceiling on the next landing and Erika wondered if he was going to jump like that on every landing.

Amelia chattered and giggled, but Erika only nodded. She hated the stairs. She hated Jesse's constant jumping. Then she thought Amelia might hang out with her old friends if Erika kept too much to herself. She flashed back to Billy's words, "Forget yourself and have fun." At the next stair-corner she laughed and jumped. "What do you think? I touched the ceiling too."

"Good job, Erika! Do you play basketball in America?" Michael playfully pulled on her braid as he took the backpack she'd been carrying.

"Yes." Without warning her homesickness hit

her. *Where did that come from?* Erika wondered, *especially when I wasn't even thinking about basketball?* Suddenly she really wanted to be home, playing basketball with Billy on the driveway. *Jesus, help me!* she prayed in desperation. By the time the group hit the street level and headed for the campus store, the sadness lifted.

Strong smells of paper, toiletries and opium fragrance soap assaulted Erika's nose as the foursome entered the China University store. She sneezed.

"God bless you!" Jesse said.

Amelia's eyebrows shot up. "God bless you? What is the occasion?" she asked.

"Just an expression that people use. Some people were afraid of evil spirits and they thought they could say, 'Bless you' after someone sneezed."

"But we don't have to be afraid—" A loud crash cut Michael's comment short, and everyone jumped.

"What the—" Erika stared around at the pots and pans scattered all over the floor. "What happened?"

"Sorry, I stepped back into the pots and pans display." Jesse bent to pick them up and lost his balance, tumbling headlong into the pile. "Oh my!" Giggles.

The store clerk appeared on the other side of Jesse and the pans. He grabbed the teen's arm and screamed at him in Chinese.

"I cannot understand you." Jesse held his hands palm up. "I'm Korean, not Chinese. I cannot understand you."

Erika jumped and everyone else looked startled as Mr. Clerk started in, even louder than before, waving his hands and jumping up and down until Gloria suddenly appeared beside him. At sight of Gloria, he quickly changed his tone and appeared to be apologizing for his tantrum.

"Mama! Where did you come from?" Amelia cried.

"I am glad I was here, buying some pencils that Monica needed," Gloria said, and turned to Mr. Clerk. Jesse, Michael and Erika picked up the pans as Amelia rearranged them on the display rack.

Gloria's quiet tone calmed everyone. Soon Mr. Clerk returned to his post behind the cash register as Gloria and the others finished their shopping.

The girls settled on a round lip-gloss tube with a brush on a wand because they couldn't find Erika's favorite brand in a small jar.

"Next time I will buy the one with shimmer," Amelia said as they headed for the cash register.

"Me too," Erika agreed, "or grape flavor. I love grape."

Half an hour later the foursome pushed through the crowd of children waiting for them in the Guesthouse lobby. Erika wanted to escape to her room. How could she endure all these swarms of children?

"Hi, kids. Ready for a game of kickball?" Michael handed Monica's backpack to Erika.

"Yes!" Every child yelled. Erika's ears buzzed. Jesse wiped the sweat off his face with his shirt-sleeve and raced to his room to fetch the ball.

Erika and Amelia met him clattering back down, bouncing the ball on each step, dripping sweat on the stairs. Erika was sure she'd have a headache if she only had time.

Both girls applied lip-gloss. Amelia smelled the contents of her cherry-scented tube for the who-knows-how-many times.

They climbed the steps to Erika's room and she dropped Monica's backpack on her bed. "I need a shower before we go to your apartment," she said, grabbing an orange top and green khaki walking shorts out of her dresser drawer.

Amelia picked up Erika's laptop and turned it on. "Nice."

"Thanks. Hey, why don't you email my twin brother Billy? I haven't told him anything about China." Amelia had everything set up before Erika could walk to her chair. "Ooooh! Wow! You must know a lot about computers."

"Yes. I love computers. You are a twin?"

"Yes, but Billy doesn't look like me. He's short, pudgy, brown hair, a computer whiz like you."

"What do Americans call us, computer geeks?"

"Yes. Or nerds." Erika decided she would not say that Billy was pimply. She disappeared into the bathroom. Then she stepped back out and set the toilet paper on the dresser. "Do you have to hide the toilet paper at home when you shower, too?" she asked, flashing back to her shock that there were no shower curtains in China. "Water splashes everywhere, over the toilet and the walls."

"Yes." Amelia barely answered because she was writing her message. "And it takes two hours for the water to drain."

"Same here."

Fifteen minutes later, Erika stepped out of the bathroom. "I'm fresh for the moment and it feels good."

"Great. I've written to Billy." Amelia looked around. "Do you have the cord to plug into the internet port and we will send it now."

"The port is downstairs. I'll send it tomorrow morning after I write a note too."

The teenagers linked arms down the steps and Erika steered Amelia into the dining room. "I need to find Monica and tell her I'm leaving. We can eat here if we want to."

"Are you hungry?" Amelia asked.

"Yeah, come to think of it, I am, a little," Erika replied.

Amelia and Erika sat next to Monica and Martin and greeted the other team members around the table.

Everyone talked at once: "Look, we have noodles and fish again."

"Amelia, can you eat with us?"

"Erika, did you see your favorite, watermelon?" Monica waved her chopsticks at the huge bowl of fresh fruit.

"Yum! Watermelon! Amelia, please eat with us." Erika reached for some chopsticks and handed a pair to Amelia.

"Sure." She glanced at her watch. "My parents

will not care as long as I am home by 6:30 p.m."

Michael led the prayer of thanks.

"China is so much safer than America," Cheryl said, searching around for her chopsticks on the table until Daniel handed them to her. "Chinese children have more freedom than Americans and Amelia can stay here without causing her parents any worry."

"And children haven't learned lots of bad ways from television and movies." Michael took a bite of peach. "It's actually acceptable for boys to hold hands when they're walking together and for girls to link arms."

The teens ate a few bites of food and then Erika scooted her chair out. "May we be excused, please? We need to go."

"How far is it?" Michael asked.

"It is just two blocks from here in the professors' apartments. My mother is Gloria, your helper with the English classes." She and Michael shook hands. "I have not met you before, Michael, although we know Miss Wen Jing and Daniel and Cheryl because we lived in Seneca while my father studied for his degree."

"We love Gloria and Ralph!" Daniel's smile split his suntanned face.

"We'll be back in time to walk with you to English Corner." Erika and Amelia chattered as they headed out the door.

* * *

Monica smiled at the girls' backs as they left.

Then she turned to Martin. "We have to get you baptized in my bathtub upstairs before we go to English Corner. I'm a licensed pastor and I can baptize you." She cleared her throat to get everyone's attention and said, "Team, just before dinner, Martin repented of running his own life and asked Jesus to run it for him. Isn't that wonderful?"

"Yes!" The team clapped and hugged him. Martin smiled so wide a dimple appeared in his left cheek.

Daniel assisted Cheryl as she rose from her chair. "We can be there in about fifteen minutes."

Michael stood up. "Robert and Jesse, we'll be there in five, right?"

"Okay."

"Martin, I'll bring you some dry clothes," Michael said as he headed upstairs with Robert.

"Thank you, Michael," Martin said with a little hand wave of appreciation.

Jesse took the steps two at a time again.

Monica stacked the dirty dishes for the server and held out her cup for a refill when Luo Yang walked by. "Thank you, Luo Yang." Yang tipped his head slightly and poured. "Do you need more tea, Martin?"

"Yes, please."

"Martin, I'd like to hear about your life, how you grew up and became a college professor."

He sat for a moment, studying his cup. "I was the youngest of a poor family with all sisters but me. My parents could not pay for my school, but I asked lots of questions and my sisters finally agreed to bring me into the classroom. I hid in the corner and listened and my sisters helped me do homework in the evenings. Then one day the teacher found me. He picked me up and set me on the sidewalk outside the school.

"Never come back," he said and dusted off his hands as if he had gotten rid of me, but I cried and stood outside the window looking in. The teacher finally realized how much I wanted to learn and said, 'Okay, we will test you and see if you can come for free.'"

"Free? Isn't God good? He helped you get a free education." Monica raised her hands in praise to God.

"Yes, my scores were so high the officials made arrangements for me to go through all the grades at the government's expense. I agreed to do what they told me, and now I have earned my Ph. D., I am 35 years old and I have advanced as far as I can."

"You speak English very well. And I was impressed with the way you answered questions in the class this afternoon."

"I still study hard and read everything I can get my hands on. I found the name 'Martin' in a book I was reading and liked it. I ask everyone to call me Martin."

"I like your name. What is the meaning?" Monica checked her watch.

"Seeker of truth."

"That fits you." She slid her chair back and led the way upstairs. She had the key in the door when

Martin whispered, "I do not want to stay here as a teacher at the University. Would you help me get over to Canada? You keep saying we can do anything we want to do."

Monica said nothing as the significance of his question sank in. She knew she shouldn't take sides and work against the government. They'd spent a lot of money getting this young man an education and now he wanted to leave China. Silently she prayed, *Lord, what do I do?*

"If you will carry the papers to America and send them to Canada, I will not ask you to do anything else," he said.

She turned the question over in her mind as they walked into her room. "Yes," she whispered, "I will carry papers, but I will not do anything else. I believe God will bless that, but I cannot help you in any other way."

"Good enough. I will start preparing the papers." They held the secret in their hearts as they stood in the doorway and welcomed the others coming for the baptism.

* * *

"Werroorrooowoooo," Monica mimicked the sound that whistled into the room. "The hidden microphone is working." She chuckled and bent over the bedside stand. "Jesus loves you," she said into the phone.

Michael joined her and explained Jesus to the listener on the other end.

"Monica is fearless," Daniel whispered to the

other team members around him. "I mean, it's amazing. She's kind of like the stereotypical dumb blonde. She pretends she doesn't understand what the Chinese police and guards are saying, but she's smart and absolutely fearless."

Cheryl grinned. "We want everyone to hear about Jesus, even the microphone tech."

— 15 —

ENGLISH CORNER

"There you are! We would have waited for you, you didn't have to run." Michael patted the panting girls' shoulders and reached for the tissues Cheryl held out. "How far did you run?"

"Only half a block, but I'm soaked from running in this heat." Erika wiped her face and craved a shower. "I'm all slimy now."

"Me too," Amelia puffed under her wad of tissues.

"Did you have fun?" Monica started to walk between them with an arm around each girl's shoulder, but she quickly dropped her arms. "Ohhhh, you *are* slimy."

Monica's arm around Erika felt good, even for a second or two. Daddy had hugged her a lot. No... . no... . she wouldn't cry.

"Amelia's family has the same cooling unit we have in our classroom. It felt good." Erika hoped her voice sounded okay, not weepy.

"Professor Bing has one at his house, too. Very nice," Monica said. The threesome kept in step past the market. Both girls applied lip-gloss and Erika looked up to see Monica smiling as she watched them. They mimicked the Chinese and bowed their heads slightly toward one another, and laughed.

"Amelia's room is really cool, all green and white. And she let me use her pink nail polish. See?"

"Oh, that's beautiful." Monica pulled Erika's hands close for a better look. "I'm glad you had a good time." Monica leaned in and said quietly, "After Cultural Lectures, Martin repented of running his own life and asked Jesus to be Lord. We baptized him in my bathtub."

Erika and Amelia both slapped the new convert a high five. Then they linked arms behind Monica and she moved up to walk with Martin.

"Tomorrow I will bring my wife." Martin's wet hair dripped down the blue shirt Michael had loaned him.

"You have a wife? We should have invited her to your baptism." Michael grabbed a wad of tissues and wiped his face.

"I did not know she could come. Her name is Joan. She teaches at CU too." Martin ran his fingers through his hair. "We have an eight-year-old daughter we call Melody."

"I'm anxious to meet them, and you gave them such lovely names." Monica did a little skip of happiness right there on the street.

Martin's reply faded into the greetings from the high schoolers, college students and professors waiting at the English Building.

"I miss the children in the evening," Monica said, "but we'll have lots of fun tonight, anyway."

I don't miss them. She hoped her double deodorant would hold. She grinned at Amelia, applying lip-gloss as she climbed the stairs.

Jesse pointed to the bulbs above the top landing, 15 stories up. "Those tiny light bulbs in the ceiling look like stars in the sky."

"You're right, Jesse," Michael said. "Which reminds me, I haven't seen the stars in the sky since I left Seneca. We have too many city lights here to see real stars."

* * *

Fifty to seventy-five people crammed into the room with the cooling unit. Michael and Jesse checked off names from Monday night and handed out nametags.

Erika squinted up at the bright lights in the ceiling. She and Amelia waved to Carol, Elizabeth and Marion sitting cross-legged on the floor in front.

Mr. Robert stood to his full six-foot height. "Good evening, ladies and gentlemen."

"Good evening, Mr. Robert," a few responses trickled back.

"I said, 'Good evening, ladies and gentlemen.'"

"Good evening, Mr. Robert," the entire group chorused together.

"That's better." Mr. Robert cleared his throat. "We're so glad to be here in China, and we're glad you came to English Corner." He laid his hand on Spy Man, fidgeting in his chair.

Erika checked her nail polish and smiled.

"Let's pray." Robert prayed, thanking God for the evening and the people who had gathered. Then he asked God to guide the class activities that evening.

Erika knew she shouldn't talk to Amelia about Spy Man until she knew her better. *I wish I'd grown up in a Christian home like Amelia did,* she thought. *But I'm still not sure she can keep a secret.*

"Our first question this evening is, 'In your idea, what is love?'" Michael wrote the question on the board. "We will divide into six groups tonight, as we did last night. Move your chairs into circles and wait for a team leader."

Erika tried hard to paste a smile on her face, hoping it didn't look too phony. She was so tired and hot. If only she were home, kicked back in Daddy's recliner, watching a movie with Billy.

Amelia, Carol, Elizabeth and Marion joined Monica's circle. Erika hid a smile as the other girls watched Amelia apply lip-gloss. She could tell they were asking questions as they inspected Amelia's round tube.

Look out, world. Here come three more lip-gloss users, she thought. Erika grinned at Amelia. "Save me a spot," she said as she waved to Martin and his wife, sitting down in the circle.

"This is my wife Joan," Martin said as Erika bowed her head slightly and reached out to shake hands with the lovely lady.

Erika raced to hand out water to the team members, and paper and pencils for taking notes.

She wouldn't take any water because Amelia couldn't have any. There was only enough for the team members tonight.

"Will you walk with me to the bathroom?" Erika turned to see Cheryl's sweet smile turned her way.

"Sure, I need to go there too." The twosome threaded their way past all the people to the hallway. She and Cheryl walked arm in arm past the two Communist guards and Erika pushed the door open. "Look, the bathrooms are nearly as dark as the hall."

"I can't see either way," the lovely lady said. Erika didn't reply because she already knew that.

Back in the circle, Erika dropped into the chair beside Monica just as she said, "I've noticed that in China, love is conditional. If you do this or that for your father, mother or teacher, they will love you… ."

"Miss Wen Jing, what does 'this or that' mean?" Spy Man crossed and uncrossed his legs.

Monica smiled into his eyes. "Oh, I'm sorry, I used an idiom without thinking about it. What does 'this or that' mean?" She looked around the circle.

"'This or that' in this case means whatever the father, mother or teacher wants done, whatever would please him or her." Martin's voice carried over the classroom and Erika remembered he was a professor, used to speaking to classrooms full of students.

"Very good, Martin." Monica smiled at several individuals sitting around the room. "Usually, in China, if you don't do what your parents or teacher want, they let you know it's not possible for them to love you."

She opened her Bible. "God's idea of love is entirely different," she said. "The Bible says God loved humans so much he sent his Son Jesus to pay the penalty for our sins. We can show this love, too, not that we're all going to die for someone. The Holy Spirit helped Jesus pay the penalty out of love and he can help us love people too."

"Maybe love does not always come with strings attached?" Martin looked thoughtful.

Amelia raised her hand. "I have never heard of 'strings attached'."

"Another idiom." Monica seemed to think hard for a second and then her eyes sparkled. She pointed to her tennis shoe. "This shoestring is a good example because it's used to tie the front of the shoe together over the tongue. In our idiom, parents or teachers use their love to tie their children to them."

Erika watched every head nod and ten mouths form circle shapes. "Oh, oh, oh."

"Are there different kinds of love?" Monica's eyes sparkled as she looked around the circle and turned to 1 Corinthians 13. Everyone sat thinking for a moment until Martin's wife Joan raised her hand. "Yes, there is parents' love."

"And love for our friends," Amelia interrupted.

"And there's love for God," Erika chimed in.

Monica patted her hand and Erika knew she'd made her mentor proud. She smiled and crossed her arms as Monica continued, "In the Bible it says, if we do things for others and have no love, it doesn't get us anything in God's favor. Only God can show us how to love. We'll talk more about that another time."

Monica checked her watch and signaled the other group leaders. "I enjoyed our discussion tonight. I like the way you are all speaking English." Then she said, "Let's move our chairs back to their original places."

Soon she stood in front of the entire group.

Erika collected the empty water bottles, the pencils and any leftover paper before she dropped onto the floor next to her friends.

Monica raised her arms and said, "Did you enjoy your discussion tonight?" Many nodded yes, but Spy Man frowned and looked at the floor. She lowered her arms and gently shook her finger at the class. "Remember that God loves you with no strings attached." Then she chuckled and pointed to Amelia. "What does 'strings attached' mean?"

Erika wondered if "putting someone on the spot" was an idiom. She twizzled her braid as Amelia stood up, explained to the group and plopped down again, all out of breath.

"Thank you, Amelia, you did a good job." Then Monica asked, "How many of you are married?" Several people raised their hands. "But if you're not married today, you're going to love someone someday." Giggles from every part of the room. "Tonight let's talk about what is the ideal person."

"She has to cook." Giggles.

"He must like children." Giggles.

"I must love her as God loves me." Martin grabbed Joan's hand and his eyes sparkled as if he had experienced a new thought.

"Very good, Martin. Yes, forgiveness is freedom. God loves us without any strings attached. He forgives those who repent of running their own lives, and we become part of God's family... ."

Ooooo! *There's that forgiveness word again*, Erika thought. She zoned out everything else and thought about Daddy's killers and Mom's abuse of Billy and herself. How could she ever forgive the people who had done so much wrong against her?

* * *

Everyone left for home around ten. "You are really quiet, Erika." Amelia watched her friend as they walked toward the Guesthouse under the street lights.

"Sorry, Amelia, I'm thinking about something I have to decide about. I'll talk more tomorrow."

"Okay." Amelia left her alone then and talked to Jesse and Michael.

At the Guesthouse, Michael glanced at Erika and said, "Jesse and I will walk with you to your apartment, Amelia." Erika watched as they jogged the first half block until Jesse tripped over his own feet and went tumbling into a flowerbed.

Now Erika could think more about forgiveness without the others around. She spotted Monica in the dining room with a table full of people from English Lecture. "I'm headed upstairs for a shower," she called and Monica waved and smiled.

Daniel, Cheryl, Michael and Robert were already deep into discussions at their own tables. Erika waved to Professor Bing at Robert's table. He tipped his head slightly and smiled.

Then she spotted tea server Luo Yang at Monica's table. She'd tell Billy about how tea servers carry boiling hot tea from table to table and reach over the diners' shoulders to fill their cups. *Monica says they're really proud of their work and good tea servers get lots of honor*, she thought, *and this one attends English Corner, too*.

Upstairs, Erika flung open the door and whined, "Ooooh." As the heat and humidity from the room almost bowled her over. She checked all the windows and found them open. She'd leave the door open between the rooms, but she'd feel like a roasted hot dog by morning without a breath of fresh air.

— 16 —

THE SPELLING BEE

The sun peeked into Erika's room the next morning as something crawled across her nose. A fly! She snapped it off. "Flies! I hate 'em." Visions of the fly-covered food at the market almost made her gag.

What a way to wake up. She heard Monica singing *Amazing Grace,* then a knock on the door between their rooms.

"Come in." Yawn.

"Good morning! Did you rest well? I was just thinking that I'm so glad you came with me to China."

Erika felt a pinkish glow start in her heart. "Good morning, Monica, my angel. I still think China is weird, but I love being with you."

Monica kissed Erika's cheek. They hugged and the glow flowed all over. "Pretty soon you'll love China as much as I do, but right now I need a big favor. I made this list from the words we've studied in the morning classes. If you type it, Gloria will have copies made and we'll give one to everyone who comes to Cultural Lectures."

"Okay. Shower first?"

"That's fine. Bring it when you pick me up for breakfast. And thank you so much for doing that." Monica disappeared into her room as Erika set the toilet paper on the dresser.

Twenty minutes later, she started typing the list and found the printer cord in her dresser drawer. While the list printed, she pulled up Amelia's message to Billy.

Billy, I'm one of the students in Monica and Erika and Michael's class. She told me to write you while she takes a shower.

It's 5:45 in the afternoon on Wednesday. We are going to my family's apartment before we go back to English Corner at 7:15.

Erika says you're a computer geek like me. We don't call each other CGs in China because computer experts receive great honor. Computers are my first love, after my parents, of course.

I'll check out Seneca, Kansas when I get home this evening. Population 100,000? Erika already gave me your street address. I know a lot about Seneca because I lived there with my parents while my dad got his college degree.

My family lives in an apartment on the China University campus in Nanchong, fourth floor. Do you Google Earth? We're next to the big flowerbed with a Buddha statue.

You'll see the Guesthouse just two blocks from my family's apartment.

Erika is ready to go. I have a web cam. Do you? My email address is LF4j@chinanet.com. You probably know "4j" means "for J___." Erika says you know J____ too. Awesome!

Later, Amelia

Erika sighed and started her own message.

Dear Billy, it's ol' lonesome me at 7:00 a.m. this morning lol J. Monica and Amelia make life bearable here, otherwise it's pretty awful. I'm still waiting for ya to write again, more than ten words, please :P?

Last night in English Corner we talked about forgiveness and it hit me like a brick, as Daddy used to say J. Monica said holding unforgiveness is like having a bird fly over and drop a blob on your nose. The bird will fly away and you'll hafta decide whether ya wanna clean the blob off yourself or leave it there forever. She said she felt so much better when she cleaned up her nose. I'm working on blob removal this morning. How are you doing with the forgiveness thing?

Professor Bing invited Monica and me to a restaurant Saturday night. I hope we don't hafta eat those cute little puppies we see in the market every day L. Or worse. Michael said it could be snake or sea slugs or chicken feet or duck brain. Sick :P!!!! I'm really not feelin' the food here buddy.

We're praying for Mom and you. Hang in there Bro.

Love ya lots, Erika

PS: Tell Mom I said "hi." See, I'm working on forgiving her. Monica says I have to be willing anyway.

She carried her laptop to breakfast, after she'd recited the first five verses of Psalm 91 to Monica.

The team followed the same class routine as on Monday and Tuesday. Erika's pink glow flamed each time a team leader thanked her for her help. Just before noon, she noticed Amelia applying lip-gloss and remembered that she'd forgotten to put on anything or check her manicure since breakfast. Hmmmm. She'd been too busy to remember, but she hadn't had time to think about forgiveness, either.

* * *

In the afternoon, Erika, Jesse and Amelia raced up the last four flights of stairs before Cultural Lectures. "Jesse won." The girls dropped down in front of the cooling unit and Jesse paper toweled his sweaty head.

"Aren't you glad your hair is so stinking short?" Erika twirled her braid.

Jesse got horizontal beside the girls. "Oh yeah,

how do you put up with long hair?"

Erika raised her nose and squinted her eyes. "Very carefully."

Amelia adjusted her pink hairclip. "Mine is short."

Jesse laughed and raced to his parents' classroom and back with bottles of water from Daniel's pack. "We need to help set up."

He gave the girls their water just as Monica handed Amelia a box of red, white and blue pencils. "The professors work as hard as the students to win these pencils. Let's put plenty of them in that jar over there."

Amelia filled the jar to capacity.

Michael gave every student a spelling list before class started, and the room grew quiet as the students studied. He opened Cultural Lectures at 3:00 p.m. with prayer, and then the group squealed, clapped and danced to the songs they'd learned.

"Jesse, do a drum roll on that chair," Michael called.

Jesse used his hands for a long, loud one and Michael announced, "Time for a spelling bee!" Erika covered her ears to shut out the noise as the students showed their delight at having a spelling bee. Michael pointed to his right, in front of the cooling unit. "Please line up over here if you want to take part."

Thirty-five contestants from high school level to college professor lined up. They breathed deep and soaked in the cool air blowing over their legs and backs as they moved past the cooler, awaiting their turn.

"Please don't feel sad if you lose today because some of you know English better than others," Michael said. "We'll divide into smaller groups when we know you better, and we'll include the younger children next time."

Sighs of relief filled the room. *The younger children really wanted to be in the bee this afternoon*, she thought. *But they wouldn't be able to compete against the older students.*

Monica stood in front and pulled a piece of paper with a word printed on it out of a basket. As usual, she slowly pronounced the word twice and told its meaning. Those who spelled a word correctly received a prize pencil and went to the end of the line for another turn. Contenders who missed their word sat down. In the end, Amelia and Martin were the last two contestants standing.

"Your turn, Amelia." Monica stood like a statue after she pulled another paper out of the basket. The cooling unit buzzed in the quiet. Amelia twisted the small gold ring on her pinky finger and rubbed her lips together as if she had just applied more lip-gloss.

"Write this word: *redemption*." Class members rolled their eyes and made hand signals to their friends.

"Re? What?" Amelia turned to the board and picked up the marker.

"Redemption." Monica gave the meaning, as usual. "This word means a person becomes a child of God by Jesus' death on the cross and resurrection." Everyone frowned because they did not understand this word or its meaning, but Monica said, "You'll understand more of the meaning after you've seen the *Jesus* movie Saturday."

"Listen to the word parts." Monica pronounced the word again, slowly: "re-demp-tion."

Amelia tugged on the hair behind her ear as she concentrated.

"Write *re*,'" Monica said, and Amelia wrote *re*.

"demp." *demp.*

"tion." *shun*

Erika glanced up at the ceiling fans whirring fast to keep the air moving. The group took a collective breath and held it.

Amelia laid down the marker and turned to Monica. Whoosh! Every breath blew out at once.

Their teacher stood stony-faced for a full half minute, studying her list. Amelia fidgeted.

"Amelia, please spell the word aloud as you've written it." Monica held her gaze on the list.

Amelia's voice shook as she spelled, "r-e-d-e-m-p-s-h-u-n."

Monica put her arm around Amelia's shoulders and looked into her dark eyes. "Amelia, I'm really, really sorry, but you didn't spell it correctly. I know you're a good speller. You'll probably win another time."

Amelia's shoulders sagged and her eyes filled with tears. "I missed it? How?"

"We'll see if Martin knows how to spell it," Monica said.

"Redemption is spelled, r-e-d-e-m-p-t-i-o-n." Martin didn't look at Amelia as he spelled it correctly.

Everyone in the room clapped and cheered for Martin. Except Amelia. She sagged onto the floor beside Erika and wiped her eyes with the back of her hand. Their shoulders touched and both heads drooped.

"Michael said we shouldn't be discouraged if we lose to someone who knows English better than we do," Erika reminded her, and Amelia raised her head. A smile started at the edges of her mouth and filled in her lips. *She's smiling. That's a relief.*

Then Monica pulled a crisp new ten-dollar bill out of her pocket and held it up for everyone to see.

"Oooohhhh! Ten dollars!" Everyone pretended to hold out his hands and grab the money.

"Ten dollars is as much as most Chinese earn in one week, 80 Yuan," Michael said from his seat beside Jesse.

"This ten-dollar bill is the grand prize today." Monica waved it again and stuffed it back into her pocket. She waited a moment until the whispering and giggling stopped.

It's as if she showed them a solid gold prize, Erika thought.

Monica pulled a word out of the basket marked "Grand Prize Words," shook her head and said, "Oh my, what a word. *Antidisestablishmentarianism*. It means you are not against the government, you are for the government." Everyone in the room nodded and smiled. This word was acceptable to them.

Martin wrote the word on the board as Monica gave him the syllables, holding his forefinger under his nose as he concentrated. A-n-t-i-d-i-s-e-s-t-a-b-l-i-s-h-m-e-n-t-a-r-i-e-n-i-s-m.

The group squirmed in their seats and sent hand signals to one another. Martin rubbed out the last *e* and replaced it with an *a*. He turned to face Monica. She studied her list, without making eye contact.

Martin, please spell the word aloud as you've written it."

His voice cracked as he started spelling, "A-n-t-i-d-i-s-e-s-t-a-b-l-i-s-h-m-e-n-t-a-r-i-a—no, I mean 'e'—no, it's 'a.'" His bottom lip twisted and he bit down hard. "Ouch!" chuckles erupted across the room.

"No talking!" Michael barked.

Martin crossed his left foot over his right one and rocked on it. "'A.' I think it's 'a.'" He searched Monica's face, but she kept her eyes on the clouds outside the window. Martin finished spelling the word, "n-i-s-m."

"Ah, oh my, that's... ." Monica twisted her face, frowned and stroked her short hair. "Correct!" Her hands flew up and her face exploded into a grin.

Martin's hands arced over his head and his smile glowed bigger than his face. "I spelled it! I spelled it!" He whirled and danced across the room.

Amelia and Erika slapped him a high five and pointed to the Communist guards peeking into the room as the cheering went on and on.

Michael and the rest of the team slapped Martin's back. The children yelled, "Hooray, Hooray! He did it!"

Monica handed Martin the ten-dollar bill and the cheering started all over again. "Congratulations, you won!" she called above the hubbub and hugged him again.

Michael stopped clapping and checked his watch. Then he called, "Class dismissed!" Martin disappeared into a mob of cheering students as they surrounded him, offering him more hugs and high fives than he could possibly return.

— 17 —

CHEWING FOR JESUS

Erika and Monica stole a few minutes of together time Saturday morning. They walked around the lake on campus and sniffed the perfumed air from the flowerbeds around them. Monica relaxed in the shade, smiling and talking with everyone, especially anyone who could understand English.

Erika crossed her arms and waited to continue the conversation after each person walked on. *I wish I had Monica's enthusiasm about Jesus and Step Up To Life*.

"I hope lots of people come today to the *Jesus* film showing." Monica shooed a fly off her lips. "So far this week twenty people have made Jesus Lord of their lives."

"Yes, I know." Erika pulled her eyebrows together. She wanted to tell Monica that the baptisms in the middle of the night interrupted her sleep. Monica could run on three or four hours of rest, but Erika needed more.

She decided to let it pass. "What should I wear tonight when we go to dinner with Professor Bing?"

"Nice pants and a cotton top? I don't know, how many outfits did you bring?" Monica waved at a mother and her toddler as they walked past. The toddler stopped and stared at Monica.

She smiled at him and waved again. "Nehou?" "Nehama?" Erika smiled too, but for a different reason. She had been in China long enough to recognize the meaning of the Chinese words, "Hello, I'm very glad to meet you, how are you?" He ran screaming into his mother's arms and Monica waved a third time to mother and child as they walked on.

"Chinese children have not seen anyone with blonde hair," Monica said with a laugh. "How many outfits?"

"Four pairs of shorts, one skirt and one pair of long pants. All cotton. All cool. All coordinated to mix and match as you suggested. And this red bag goes with everything. I can't wait to get home to some different clothes. Mostly my comfy hipster jeans.

Monica abruptly changed the subject. "We need to get back to the Guesthouse for lunch and walk to the film showing with the team." Erika had trouble keeping up with her mentor on the walk back.

* * *

"They'll have a clearer picture of who Jesus is after we show *The Passion of the Christ* and *The End of the Spear*, but we'll ask how many want a copy of *Step Up To Life* today." *SUTL,* Erika thought. Monica pointed to the box of SUTLs and

Erika and Amelia passed them out. Daniel went over the little booklet with the group, and two children prayed to receive Christ as Lord.

Spy Man read along, but he didn't pray the prayer at the end. Erika chin-pointed at him behind his back and Monica grinned.

I think God is doing something in Spy Man, Erika thought.

She flashed back to Daniel's comments during their training in the United States: "There will be many times we know that our conversations are being taped on the phone, or there are officials sitting in our classrooms, listening to what we are teaching. But if we do it all under the guise of Western culture, sharing what our holidays are about, etc., sharing how the Ten Commandments were used to shape law in the Western world, etc., we will be protected."

* * *

"We need to get some Bibles to give our dear converts," Michael said on the way back to the Guesthouse.

"Let's go to one of the government churches." As they passed the market, Monica stooped to pet a chicken in its crate. "They've always helped me out before."

"How about a Sunday morning, and we can attend the service?" Michael patted a puppy in its cage.

Daniel bought Cheryl a huge bunch of flowers and gave them to her with a kiss.

"Oh, thank you, they smell so good!" Cheryl almost knocked her hat off as she stuck her nose deep into the bouquet. "Mmmm." She looked up as if she could see the sky. "I smell rain. Where's the umbrella?"

Daniel barely got it up before the downpour hit. It drenched the slower-moving umbrella launchers and quickly made a muddy mess of the sidewalk.

"I see what you meant, Monica, about walking in stuff, when you told me to wear socks with my sandals. My feet are all slimy now." Erika stepped over a mini-river flowing past the chicken merchant's stall.

"We'll use disinfectant on your feet and sandals when we get back to the guesthouse," Monica said.

"At least there isn't any lightning this time." Amelia looked up at the sky, already clearing, with a rainbow over the street. "That rainbow looks so close, I think I can touch it." She held out her hand.

Michael, Erika and Jesse pretended to catch the rainbow.

"I'll take the blue," Jesse said.

"Here, catch." Michael made a fake throw, mimicking a football player's posture.

"Toss me the lavender." Erika held out her hands and Michael pretended to tear off a piece and toss it to her.

"Throw me the—" Amelia stopped mid-sentence and the group turned to watch three policemen escorting a man out of the house where the mantou bread was sold. "He's wearing handcuffs." Tears gathered in her eyes.

"What's going on?" Erika glanced at Monica who had come back to walk with her.

"The police are arresting someone, probably a Christian," Monica said in a low voice. "Don't be so rough, he won't hurt you," she whispered as the officers shoved the man into their car and drove off. A woman and child ran out of the house into the street. "What did he do? What are the charges?" the woman cried, clutching her little boy and sobbing. The little boy, about four years old, started a high-pitched wail that echoed through the market area.

Cheryl and Daniel took a protective stance around Jesse, and the family wept together. "Probably another Christian headed for torture and forced slavery in the prison," Daniel said quietly.

Erika noticed that Michael stood close to Amelia as if he were protecting her. "Maybe an example for us to be careful?" his voice barely carried in the still air.

"Let's pray for that man." Monica held out both hands. The team gathered in a circle and closed their eyes. The children who had been walking with them stood quietly inside the circle, eyes large and round. Erika noticed Abraham clinging to his parents. Some began to weep. Daniel prayed aloud for the man and his family to be protected and comforted.

"Pray for my daddy," Joab whispered. "He is in jail because he is a Christian." Michael knelt and circled the boy into his arms. He also prayed with the other children who asked.

"We'd better get back to the Guesthouse." Monica led the group away from the market area. Michael and Jesse walked with Erika and Amelia. Robert and the Carters walked with the other children. A somber mood hung like a heavy cloud over the group as they mounted the steps and entered the Guesthouse lobby.

Michael motioned for the children to come close. "I'm sorry we cannot stay and play with you today, but the team has been invited out for dinner this evening and we have to take showers and get ready. "I will pray for you. Remember, Jesus will be with you. Talk to him if you feel afraid or lonely." He hugged each child, telling him or her to hurry home and be safe.

Team members hurried to their rooms to get ready for the evening. Abraham's parents had invited the Carters to their apartment, and Robert and Michael were going to dinner with Martin's family.

* * *

At six, Professor Bing and Cao Yu pulled in front of the Guesthouse just as Monica and Erika closed the front door and moved onto the steps.

"Hello, it's so good to see you again, Cao Yu," Monica said and Professor Bing interpreted. Yu smiled and reached from the front window to shake hands with the Americans.

Professor Bing held the car door for Monica and Erika. "We'll meet Mr. Xun, Dr. Wang and Dr. Du at the Five Lilies Restaurant." He changed to

Chinese and Erika heard her name as he pointed to her. She smiled and bowed her head slightly in her seat as Cao Yu smiled back.

"Monica, I like your hair." The professor interpreted for Yu, and Monica laughed, combing through her short hair with her fingers.

"Thank you again for helping me that first night in China," Monica said. "And the chicken dinner you cooked was delicious."

Yu smiled as the professor interpreted for her. Erika breathed deep as Yu's expensive perfume filled the car and covered the acrid smell of pollution. She held the sweet fragrance in her lungs for a few seconds before exhaling and drawing in another delicious breath.

"It will be good to see Mr. Xun and Dr. Wang and Dr. Du again," Erika said. "That trip in the van was a hoot, except for the accident." *I'll pretend I'm not nervous.*

Monica patted Erika's hand. "Everything will be okay," she whispered and Erika realized her fear of eating dog or snake was showing on her face. How could she relax when her stomach already churned?

"There they are!" Monica waved at the others, waiting by the front door. Many smiles and hand shakes later, they went inside the restaurant.

"It's so small!" Erika flashed back to the last time she parked Mom's car in the two-car garage at home. Two cars would probably fit inside this restaurant. "Are all the restaurants like this?"

"Yes," Monica whispered and Erika remembered she shouldn't criticize anything about China.

The owner greeted them with many smiles and bows. "Welcome," he said and led them to a large round table where he had placed handkerchiefs with the restaurant's name on them as favors.

Everyone in the restaurant gave Monica and Erika great honor as Americans. Professor Bing announced that Monica was a volunteer summer English teacher at China University and Erika was her assistant. Several diners rose from their chairs to shake hands. Monica smiled into their eyes, but Erika stood by the table with her arms crossed and her eyes to the floor. *I can't avoid swarms of people, even in a tiny restaurant*.

Some Chinese diners gathered around Monica and Erika realized they were practicing their English: "I have never seen, how do you say, blonde hair?" and "Your eyes are blue?"

Monica talked with each person who approached her.

I don't smell the bathroom, Erika thought. Monica had said they usually put the bathroom beside the kitchen, but not here. Whew!

Finally the guests were seated and Erika found herself between Monica and Dr. Du. "Just like in the van." She smiled at Dr. Du, but not quite into her eyes as Monica would have done. Dr. Du patted Erika's braid and asked about her new experiences. Erika answered her questions, but how could she relax when the thought of eating little puppies swirled in her head?

"I will bring you the specialty of the house,"

Owner Man said and hurried to the kitchen.

Erika wished she could ask him what he planned on serving.

A server placed a large plate of egg rolls on the table and bowls of dark brown soup with tiny dumplings.

"Wonton soup! I love it!" Monica lifted the inch-long dumplings out of the broth with her chopsticks.

Erika could do that too. She mimicked her mentor and lifted the bowl of broth to her lips for a taste. She wiped her mouth on her napkin and wished for a mocha banana smoothie and a Coke.

Monica and the others laughed and joked and tasted the appetizers while they waited for Owner Man's promised treat. Erika studied the Chinese characters on the walls and dreamed of home.

"This smells so good." Monica sniffed as Owner Man emerged from the kitchen, beaming with pride, and personally placed the bowls of food on their table.

"This is snake." He stood up straight and proud.

Erika's stomach jerked in protest. How could anyone look so proud to serve snake? Gross! Erika succeeded in pasting on a half-smile. Her stomach felt like a bowling ball swaying in a hammock.

"Oh, I've never eaten snake before. Thank you for preparing this for us." Monica placed her napkin on her lap. And right there, with everyone listening and Owner Man standing by with his proud smile, Monica said, "Let's pray before we eat. Please hold hands." She reached for her neighbors' hands and bowed her head. The other guests at the table glanced at one another. It was so quiet in the restaurant that Erika could hear the fountain bubbling in the corner. Then everyone in the room held hands and bowed their heads, too.

"Thank you, Jesus, for this food," the small woman prayed loud enough for every diner in the restaurant to hear. "Bless my friends, and help them know Jesus because he loves them so much. Amen."

Erika pretended not to notice the look of surprise and shock on Professor Bing's face as his guests raised their heads and began filling their plates with meat and sauce from a big bowl. Erika took a spoonful. She and the others spooned rice and vegetables from the other bowls onto their plates, along with another egg roll. A tea server reached over their shoulders and filled their cups.

"Erika, do you like to use chopsticks by now?" Professor Bing smiled at her and she began to relax.

"I can use them, see?" She lifted a bite of vegetables to her mouth just as Monica used her chopsticks to take a bite of snake. Ew! Erika swallowed hard and fast to stop the gagging before anyone heard her. Her left hand flew to the swaying hammock. With her right hand she took a tiny sip of tea.

"It tastes like chicken." Monica took another bite and Erika watched her grin at the other guests around the table, and chew.

Disgusting!

Then Monica lifted a small, gray, funny-shaped piece of meat out of the sauce on her plate.

"What could this be?" Monica held it up with her chopsticks.

"You got the snake's brain," Dr. Du said. "It is the best part."

"Brain? Maybe I'll be smarter if I eat this snake's brain." Monica giggled. She popped the gray blob into her mouth, chewed, and grabbed a drink of tea. She smiled at Cao Yu as she swallowed.

Erika gulped. *I hope my face hasn't turned green*. She picked up more rice and vegetables in her chopsticks and shoved them into her dry mouth. Then a wonderful thought flashed in her mind: *Monica said it's poor manners to eat everything on your plate in China*. Thank goodness! Saved from eating snake by the etiquette book! She wanted to drop her napkin over the entire plate and pretend this dinner never existed.

Erika laughed out loud and let go of the hammock when Owner Man set a huge plate of fresh oranges and Jasmine tea on the table for dessert.

Afterward, she succeeded in shaking hands with everyone and smiling on the way out the door. The cool night air and Cao Yu's perfume soothed her as she climbed into Professor Bing's back seat.

"God answered our prayers, Monica," Erika whispered. "I made it through the entire evening without gagging." The hammock feeling sneaked in for one last swing and then vanished as Monica squeezed her hand. She could hardly wait to tell Billy she almost ate snake brain.

* * *

"Thank you for such a lovely evening. We really had a great time. And I'm so glad I got to see you again, Cao Yu." Monica reached up and patted Yu's shoulder as the professor interpreted. Cao Yu smiled and patted back.

"Yes, thank you, Professor Bing." Erika crossed her arms and tried to think of something else to say.

"You are welcome. Your students seem to be glad you have come here, Erika, and the officials appreciate the good job you are doing." Erika grinned in the darkness and tried to think of something to say.

Just then Professor Bing pulled in front of the Guesthouse and got out to open their door. "By the way, we have decided to send the American team on a little outing at the end of the month. We will make travel arrangements for the destination of your choice."

"The Great Wall! The Great Wall!" Erika fought the urge to jump up and down like a 5-year-old.

— 18 —

THE GREAT WALL

Two weeks later, Monica and Erika looked down at the airport in Beijing. Erika grabbed Monica's hand and gave it a squeeze. "I won't freak out this time about the buildings being so far from where we land."

"A little experience helps."

The next morning, they joined 38 other tourists to climb aboard a rickety tour bus. "Are you sure this thing is gonna get us there?" Erika watched skeptically as the bus driver checked the oil.

"Oh sure, the bus is more capable than it looks. The Great Wall is thirty kilometers northwest. We'll make it fine."

"How far is that in miles?" Erika asked.

"About twenty miles," Monica said and turned to strike up a conversation with the lady across the aisle.

Beijing, China's capital and second largest city, stretched out behind them as they bounced along. Beautiful mountain scenery rose up on either side of the road.

At the Wall, the bus driver parked in the shade and Mr. Tom the tour guide stood up. "This is the east end of the Great Wall." He went on to explain in excellent English that everyone needed water, snacks, and good walking shoes. He pointed out a small store across the parking lot.

Half an hour later, Mr. Tom led the group to the steps at the edge of the parking lot and started the climb. "You are welcome to climb with me or go on your own."

"You've climbed this wall many times, right?" Erika noted the huge muscles bulging on his calves.

"Yes. Twice a week all summer." Mr. Tom took two more steps.

Monica donned a straw hat with a red ribbon that matched her pants. Erika's blue ball cap had once matched her washed-out blue shorts and white shirt with an American flag in front. Monica had given it to her to replace a tank top that wasn't suitable for the trip.

Erika noticed a middle-aged, overweight American couple gazing at the hundreds of steps leading up the mountainside.

"I thought it was a straight-up climb," the woman whined, "maybe thirty-five to fifty feet, and you climb that and you're at the top. My knees are killing me already."

"I am sorry about your knees." Mr. Tom pointed to an ancient fortress, far away. "You start with these steps and climb to that fort at the top. You will have to start with other sets of stairs with fortresses at the top, to reach other parts of the Wall."

Erika cringed as the woman groaned. "What have we gotten ourselves into?" Her husband stood still, gazing at all those steps.

"Our ancestors built this wall for defense and for the safe movement of troops." Mr. Tom continued his lecture. "Sometimes forts and towers in the Wall housed soldiers when needed. The regiments moved along the top of the Wall to wherever the enemy was attacking, or where someone thought the enemy would attack."

"We couldn't get on it and travel for, say, a hundred miles?" A tall, blond teenager squinted at the old fort far away. Then he put his arms around two college-age girls who stepped up beside him.

"Excuse me, I talked to you on the bus," Monica cut in. Smiling apologetically, she said, "Your name is Chad. You're on tour with a college class from America."

"Yes, UCLA." He touched the bill of his red baseball cap in a mock salute.

Mr. Tom frowned at Monica's interruption. "You can walk only in the area that has been opened up from these steps."

"Fabulous." Monica held her hat on, tilted her head and looked up. "Let's get started."

Other members of the tour group gazed at the hundreds of crude stone steps leading up. "Is that four rest areas along the way? I'll need every one of them." A thirtyish woman with a British accent moaned.

That woman looks much younger than Monica, Erika thought, and bit her tongue to keep from saying, "Watch this lady eat up those steps. You're much younger than she is, but you can't keep up with her."

"Where's the elevator?" another college student with a UCLA shirt whimpered.

"The ancients who built this wall never dreamed of elevators, and besides, this will be fun," Monica said and Erika grinned at her words.

The 90-degree heat bore down on hundreds of tourists unloading from buses and milling around the parking lot.

Erika and Monica started out with their tour group, but they soon pulled ahead of the wheezing, gasping climbers. Mr. Tom stayed with most of the group, as any tour guide worth his hiking Nikes would do.

Erika stopped when Monica smiled and attempted to encourage individuals sitting on the steps. "Isn't this fun? You need to keep moving if you intend to make it to the top." Most just mopped their foreheads, guzzled water and shook their heads.

Chad joined the pair before the first rest stop.

"Where are all of your college buddies, Chad?" Monica applied sunscreen and handed the tube to Erika.

"Maybe they used their minds so hard they forgot to work out." He snapped a picture or two with his digital camera.

"We've climbed 15 flights of steps three times

a day for a month. We're in great shape for this climb." Chad's baby blues were full of questions, and Monica continued with her explanation: "We're teaching English for The English as a Second Language China Group at China University in Nanchong this summer. The elevator repairman is on vacation and no one else can fix the elevator." Monica sipped her water.

"And she leads the group, all the way to the top step every time without stopping." Erika applied lip-gloss.

Monica moved her foot across the step in front of her. "There has to be a technique for walking these irregular steps. Would you say some are eight inches tall and some are eighteen inches or more?"

"And narrow." Chad's entire heel hung over. "My foot doesn't even fit on this one, it's six inches deep."

"Let's try this." Monica tried a sidestep, sort of like a crab-step dance, and Erika giggled and followed.

"This is cool." Chad devised his own technique.

Monica laughed at his antics. "Next thing we'll hear you climbed Mt. Everest."

"Maybe. I work out and climb mountains back home in Colorado. I'm thinking about the Big E." Chad's calf muscles rippled under his shorts.

"I'm beginning to get the rhythm here." Erika felt almost giddy at her success.

The threesome stopped at the first rest stop and munched a few rice crackers Erika pulled out of the backpack. They pointed out people from their group far below, hunched over, puffing, hanging onto the rock sidewall.

"Even Mr. Tom puffs like a blowfish."

Monica didn't answer as she headed to the benches where the tourists gathered.

Erika and Chad sipped water by the sidewall and waited. "Her bright smile dazzles everybody." He chin-pointed to Monica.

"Yep. Call her Monica the magnet." Erika felt the sidewall's rough texture under her fingers. "She talks to everybody."

They watched her dispense hugs and the small SUTLs with rainbow colors on the cover.

"What's that she's handing out?" Chad asked.

"*Step Up to Life*. It tells people about Jesus." Monica looked up once and waved. They waved back and waited. After a while she joined them.

"Two more Chinese have decided to follow Christ," she said with a grin. "Ready to climb some more?" She stuffed leftover booklets into her pocket.

"Yahoo!" Erika said and Chad gave her a quizzical look.

She walked a little behind as she listened to Chad's comment: "I've heard you talk a lot about Jesus everywhere—the hotel lobby, on the bus, and now."

"Do you know him?" Monica stopped climbing and looked deep into his eyes.

Chad adjusted his ball cap. "I went to church when I was small, but I don't know if you'd say I know him."

"I'm in China because of him." Monica laid her hand on Chad's arm for support while she took an extra high step. "He's my best friend."

Chad helped her up the step and said nothing.

"Hello, do you speak English?" A tall young Chinese man with rimless glasses and an American haircut came alongside Monica.

"Yes," Monica replied, "and you do too?"

"Yes, a little. My name is Zhang Hui. I attend China University in Nanchong. I'm here with some of my friends today."

"Nice to meet you, and you speak excellent English," Monica said and reached out her hand.

"Thank you." Zhang Hui shook her hand and smiled. "I had an American roommate last year in college."

"We're from CU too. This is my friend Erika." They bowed and returned his smile. "We're teaching with the English as a Second Language Group there."

She pointed to Chad. "Chad is traveling with an American college group and we're all here on vacation."

"UCLA." Chad and Zhang Hui shook hands.

"At least some of us are climbing, most are just tottering and puffing." Erika pointed down the steps.

Zhang Hui grinned as Monica took a deep breath to fill her lungs. She pointed to the lush green growth on the mountain. "Isn't God's handiwork wonderful?."

Erika noted that he stopped walking for a moment and stared hard at Monica when she mentioned Jesus. The sunlight glinted off his glasses as he leaned down and said quietly, "I've heard about Jesus."

Monica pulled out a SUTL and Zhang Hui glanced around. Erika wondered if he worried about who might be listening. He seemed to decide they were standing far enough away from anyone who could hear them and he would not be reported to the government authorities for talking about religions other than the state church.

"I want you to be free," Monica said. "Right now you are closed in a society that is very structured, but Jesus can set you free. This booklet will help you see how you can have the joy of living when you've invited him to take control of your life."

Zhang Hui placed the booklet carefully in his pocket and gave it a little pat. "May I walk with you?"

"You're welcome to join us, right, Chad and Erika?" Monica started the crab step dance again and the others followed.

"Sure, uh, do you have another one of those little books?" Chad held out his hand. "I'd like one too."

"Certainly." Monica reached into her pocket. "We can talk about this some more."

"Yeah. I like what I see you doing," Chad said.

"I always assume I have a green light to talk about Jesus until God gives me a red light." She handed Chad an SUTL and pointed to the Wall, snaking upward in the deep green mountain foliage. A few tourists dotted the steps ahead of them. Chad and Erika each snapped some pictures.

"This section of the Great Wall was built in the Ming Dynasty, 1400 A.D., and it's in fairly good condition." A tour guide led a group of tourists behind them.

The foursome walked over the ancient, crumbling bricks with earth pounded between them, up more steep stairs leading from one level of the mountain to the next.

Zhang Hui pointed out the peepholes along the top of the sidewalls for ancient archers to shoot arrows.

"Thank God for his beautiful handiwork," Monica said quietly. Her companions stood in silence around her. "Thank you, Father, for this beautiful creation, and these three precious young people."

Who all see Jesus in Monica, Erika thought. Her eyes filled with tears as love flooded her heart for the dear lady. She longed to have Daddy and Billy here too. She turned toward the view and brushed her eyes with the back of her hand. Maybe Zhang Hui and Chad would think it was the sun that made her eyes water.

"Horses probably walked two abreast over some of these four-foot-wide areas," Zhang Hui said.

Erika's stomach tickled when the top narrowed to only eighteen inches and she looked down at the ground so far away.

"This is the original wall." Zhang Hui opened a door for the group that led to a closed-in space.

"Oh, look, someone's been sleeping here. Do they stay overnight?" Monica lightly touched the single black hair on the pillow.

"Yes, people work as guards here, watchmen on the wall." Zhang Hui glanced at his watch. "Excuse me, I have to go back because I'm meeting my friends at eleven. I have just fifteen minutes."

"It was nice to meet you, Zhang Hui. May I give you a grandma hug?"

"Certainly." He placed his arm around Monica's shoulder and squeezed, released her and started to bow to Erika and Chad. Then he held out his hand. "Nice to meet you." They shook hands. "I hope you enjoy your tour."

The other two smiled and shook his hand.

Zhang Hui waved as he started back down the steps.

Erika grinned at Monica. "He keeps patting his pocket with the SUTL inside."

"Oh, Zhang Hui," Monica called and he stopped to squint up at her. "We're staying at the CU Guesthouse if you want to come by our hotel in Nanchong. Or come to the afternoon or evening sessions in the English Building, fifteenth floor."

"Thank you. I'll come." He waved again and resumed his reverse side straddle crawl down the steps.

"We'll be looking for you." Monica turned her gaze once more toward the horizon.

Chad took more pictures. "What's your email? I'll send you some of these photos." Erika scribbled it on a piece of notepaper from the backpack and handed it to him.

"Erika, do we still have that flag?" Monica held her hand out backward as she gazed at the beautiful mountains.

"Yes." Erika found the small American flag in the backpack and Monica poked the stick into the ground next to a large boulder.

"This is the flag of freedom," she announced, obviously not worried about those who might be listening. "I claim China for Jesus and the freedom that he gives."

Erika glanced at several tourists watching them and recalled Monica's remark, "I want to tell everyone in China about Jesus." *Even on the Great Wall*, she thought.

"I'll agree with that," Chad said and Erika nodded. An old Chinese vendor with a long beard bumped Chad with his cart and apologized with a deep bow and many Chinese words. Chad bowed and grinned at the man as he hobbled to a small flat space with his cart.

Erika gazed at all the vendors' carts crowded into any flat place that would hold one.

"How did you get your wares and your cart up here?" Monica fingered a silk scarf.

"We carry them up," the tiny woman vendor answered. "You like scarf?"

"Wow!" Erika and Chad pointed down the steps. "Carry them up? I'd use a helicopter," they said together and grinned.

"I'll buy this one." Monica paid the woman three Yuan "Look!" She pointed. "There's *John 3:16* carved into that rock over there, nice and big for everyone to see. Can you believe, someone worked hard to chisel that Bible reference into the rock."

She started quoting, loud and clear: "For God so loved the world that he gave his only begotten son, that whoever believes in him should not perish, but have eternal life."

Chad stared silently at the reference. Erika placed her hand over her heart. "That's awesome."

"John 3:16? What is meaning?" The tiny vendor asked.

"Read this, it will tell you everything you need to know." Monica handed the lady a SUTL in Mandarin. "I know you're too busy now, but you can read it later."

"Thank you, I always wondered about that John 3:16." The vendor pocketed the pamphlet and turned to her next customer.

"Now to get back down the steps without breaking our necks." Chad led the way.

— 19 —

BUS TO CHURCH

"You're back!

"Welcome!"

"How was The Great Wall?"

Monica and Erika answered every question and asked plenty of the other team members as they gathered around the table Sunday evening for supper. Other diners at the Guest House welcomed them back too.

Michael shared digital photos from the sweet bus tour the others had taken to the mountains. "We saw panda bears in their natural habitat and toured an ancient temple." Jesse made everyone laugh when he mimicked the bears in a tree.

"We'll have to wait and have our photos developed at home." Erika wished for a digital camera.

Jesse dashed upstairs and brought down the beautiful jade pieces Cheryl and Daniel bought. Robert and Michael showed their souvenirs. Monica and Erika displayed the beautiful red silk fabric they planned to have sewn into qi paos.

"Are you still wearing your red shoes?" Tea

Server Yang greeted Monica and everyone with hugs.

"These are different shoes, but they're still red." Monica wriggled her toes in her red tennis shoes. "Wasn't that a hoot when those ladies said I shouldn't be wearing red shoes?"

Yang chuckled and Monica told the story for the team members who missed it. He fingered the red silk fabric. "Monica, you said you would tell me about a Chinese woman you saw in a vision."

"Oh, yes. When I was seven, I stayed with my uncle's family and they prayed for me to become a missionary. I didn't know what *missionary* meant, but little girls didn't ask a lot of questions in the 1950s. A few minutes later I was playing with my toys and in my mind's eye I saw a lovely lady smiling at me. She had beautiful black hair and a slender figure, wearing a red qi pao.

"I said, 'Oh, that lady is Chinese.' I had never seen one in my life, but I knew she was Chinese. I thought, 'She is beautiful!' The vision faded and I didn't even mention it to anybody.

"Many years later when I went to China, the Lord brought it to my mind. Then I realized He gave me a thought about my future and how I would love China. I always wear red because that lady wore red."

Michael pointed to a tall man in the dining room doorway who appeared to be searching for someone. "Is that man looking for us?"

"Oh that's Zhang Hui!" Monica waved. "Zhang Hui, we're over here!" Monica and Erika stood up and hugged him, and then Monica introduced the other team members. "We're so glad you could come this evening! It's good to see you!"

"The desk clerk said he thought you were in here. I'm glad I found you." Zhang Hui served himself some rice and watermelon after the server brought a plate and chopsticks. He pulled the SUTL out of his pocket and asked many questions and listened to Monica's explanations. "I'll think about it," he said when Monica asked him to make Jesus the one god in his life and turn away from all others. "And I'll see you tomorrow evening in English Corner."

Erika inhaled the perfume from her cuticle cream. That night she emailed Billy,

Ten days till we leave for home!!!!!!

And he emailed back,

Okay, hurry up, will ya? It's really quiet around here and I hate to write ANYTHING, even to my favorite twin sister. I'll tell ya what's going on when ya get here. John's a good friend, but he's not you, and I miss ya, Kid. Mom hasn't changed much. Gotta go. Wrestling practice. Love ya lots, Billy

"Thanks for nothing," she muttered after she read the short note. She wondered if he really hated to write like he said, or was it just an excuse for not communicating?

Friday in English Corner, Monica repeated the same message she'd given in the daytime classes: "Everyone is invited to church on Sunday."

Erika yawned behind her hand and scowled. The announcement was already drummed into her head.

"We will meet you on the corner at 9:00 a.m. Sunday morning." Monica closed the session with prayer and everyone trooped toward the door, laughing and talking about the fun they'd had doing the Chinese chicken dance. The girls chattered about the American wedding Monica said they would role play next week.

"She promised we'd have a bride and groom, bridesmaids, flower girls and everything, just like an American wedding," a beautiful college student said.

Erika flashed back to Monica's explanation: "We teach the importance of love and commitment in marriage while we're having a lot of fun."

Zhang Hui looked through Monica's name book and chose the American name Steven. He walked back to the Guesthouse with the team. They discussed the meaning of his name, "blessing," over dinner.

"I'm still thinking about it," Steven said when Monica asked him to repent of running his own life and commit to Christ.

"I hope you don't think we're pushing you," Monica said, "but we're leaving for America in a few days and you need to make your decision soon."

Zhang Hui flipped through the name book

again and made no comment.

"I have to call Charlotte back home." Monica pulled her phone card out of her pocket. "She prays for me and I need to give her a report, especially about Zhang Hui, er Steven." Erika stayed with Amelia and the team around the table.

On Saturday the team showed *The Passion of the Christ* DVD. In the evening they went to a restaurant as Gloria and Ralph's guests.

At the restaurant, Erika managed to get through the meal of boiled duck heads without gagging. She came close, though, when Amelia dug out the eyes with her chopsticks and chewed them as if they were apple pie.

She didn't ask Amelia to go along to the bathroom because she had to leave the table in a hurry after Ralph used a knife to saw through his duck's skull and pulled out the brain. He dipped it in peanut sauce, popped it into his mouth and grinned with delight as he chewed. Erika made her quick getaway from the table, but she flew out of the cubicle without flushing when a man entered the stall next to her.

Back at the table, Monica whispered, "Is everything okay?" and Erika told her about the man in the bathroom

"He was talking to himself and I knew by his voice that he was a man." Erika twisted her fingers together and glanced at the man rounding the corner from the bathroom.

"In China, men and women usually use the same restroom," Monica whispered back. "Not at the airports and other large buildings but at smaller businesses like this one." She squeezed Erika's hand "I'm sorry, I should have warned you."

"USA, I long for you!" Erika muttered under her breath.

* * *

Saturday evening they baptized ten new believers in Monica's bathtub. Erika had heard the students praying to receive Christ late Friday night. She hoped the Communist official listening through the phone heard their message.

On Sunday morning, Erika, Monica and the team walked to the corner. She missed Amelia because her parents took her to the secret church.

"I want to go with Amelia to her church," Erika had said last night.

"If we Americans went to a secret church, the police would follow us and arrest the Chinese believers they found there," Monica said. "You know they wouldn't arrest us, but our presence would be dangerous for the Chinese."

"And they would go to prison for a long time." Erika repeated what Monica had told her before they left the U.S.

"Oh, look! There must be thirty or forty people waiting to go with us! And I see Martin and Steven!" Monica and the team hugged everyone and greeted them by their American name. Everyone tipped their heads slightly to Xun Man where he stood under a tree, and he responded with small bows. "Are you going with us, Mr. Xun?"

"Yes."

Erika listened as Monica chatted with him. "When can we meet and talk about the reasons you need Jesus in your life?"

"We've already talked about it." Xun Man looked past Monica to a bird in the tree.

"But I want you to understand completely. Maybe I could meet you for lunch near your office," Monica suggested. Erika knew Monica could be extremely persistent, and she wasn't surprised that her mentor insisted.

Erika flashed back to Monica's statement: "The people might not even hear the name of Jesus after the team leaves for America, let alone make a decision to follow him."

"I'll think about it." Mr. Xun looked at the sky, not at Monica.

"There's the bus." Everyone climbed aboard and sat together in a block of seats for the one-hour ride to the government church.

Monica led songs about Jesus they'd learned in the classes. Loud. So passersby on the street could hear. Michael took pictures.

The bus group crowded into the church with about three hundred other people. Pastor Meng Xiaofeng, a young, droning employee of the state, spoke Chinese for two hours, as if he were trying to convince his listeners about something. *He doesn't even have a Bible on the podium*, Erika thought. *Monica said they often use the church service to teach Communist ideas*.

Erika inspected her cuticles and thought about

home, and her dilemma. *Where does real forgiveness come from?* How would she ever be able to forgive Daddy's killers and Mom? She wished she could apply lip-gloss. The perfume from her Code Pink body wash soothed her senses. A cute toddler in the seat next to her stared at her hair without blinking.

Every visitor received a Bible after the service and an invitation to return next Sunday. *This is silly*, Erika thought, *they hand out Bibles but Monica says they preach Communism*. Erika resolved to maintain a silent, polite attitude. *Monica would like that*, she thought.

Then Pastor Meng invited the visitors to attend a banquet in an adjoining room. "I wondered what that delicious smell was," Jesse said.

After the meal, Jesse groaned, "Oh, I'm so full!" Michael grinned and stretched.

"You look sleepy enough for a nap," Erika said, and Michael made a few snoring sounds next to her ear.

Thank God, she didn't have to eat the eyes and the brain. "I keep hearing *bola*. Does that mean full?"

"Yes." Michael and Jesse spoke together and grinned.

"May we buy 100 more Bibles? We've had more converts and we need every Bible we can buy." Monica looked into Pastor Meng's eyes without even trying to speak quietly. Erika glanced at Xun Man, the powerful Communist Party Secretary, sitting across the table.

"I don't have any now." Pastor Meng glanced around at the staring eyes. "But I can get some by Wednesday."

Monica and Michael hugged the pastor gently. Erika dug her lip-gloss out of her bag and wondered how Monica and the other adults could hug everybody, regardless.

"I see you're wearing a sling. Did you hurt your shoulder?" Michael gently touched Pastor Meng's arm.

"Yes, somebody crashed into my bicycle and I fell."

"I'm sorry you were hurt," Monica said.

"May we pray for you?" Pastor Meng nodded yes, but looked doubtful. Monica and Michael prayed loud enough for everyone to hear, asking God to take away the pain, injury and stiffness in his shoulder.

He thanked them and glanced around.

"How does your shoulder feel?" Michael asked.

Pastor Meng's eyes grew large as he moved his arm and twisted his shoulder. "It doesn't hurt any more!"

Erika grinned behind her fan at Xun Man's open-mouthed stare.

"May I pray and thank God for healing you?" Monica asked. Pastor Meng nodded and she started a long prayer with the message from SUTL folded up in the words... .

"Amen," Michael said when she finished and hugged the pastor one more time. Pastor Meng returned a tight, two-arm hug.

Everybody boarded the bus for home, with Michael leading the songs all the way.

Erika sat quietly without making conversation because she had a lot to think about on the ride back to the Guesthouse. She watched Monica, though, and hoped her eyes would twinkle like Monica's someday. She thought about the service. *I missed the warm feeling I usually get in a church service*, she thought. She was surprised at a desire to pray for Pastor Meng and the congregation. *Bless them with the knowledge of you,* she prayed. *Let them know you in the way that's described in the Bible.*

Suddenly Monica leaned over, coughing violently.

"What's wrong?" Michael dropped to one knee and looked into her red, tear-streaked face.

"A bug," she wheezed. "I swallowed a bug." She took a glug from her bottle of water and rubbed her throat. Slowly the coughing stopped.

"A bug?"

"She swallowed a bug?" echoed through the bus.

Monica wiped her eyes and blew her nose after all that coughing. "Yes, it came in this window and down my throat so fast I didn't know what happened. It was crawling and scratching and trying to get out while I coughed. The water helped. Ugh! What a feeling!"

"Ugh!" "Ugh!" The Chinese had learned another new word.

Erika gulped her own water and hoped her

stomach would settle down. She wouldn't even think about Monica getting sick from that creepy bug. Not cool. Not cool at all.

Conversation buzzed again when everyone knew Monica was okay.

*   *   *

On Wednesday, Erika, Monica and Michael made the long trip back to the church. "We are here for the Bibles." Monica pulled out her Chinese money. "Oh, hello, Mr. Xun, I didn't know you would be here."

"Hello." Xun Man stood up from the chair in Pastor Meng's office and shook their hands. Then he sat back down.

"I am very sorry," Pastor Meng said, glancing at Xun Man, "but I found only three."

"Three? but we need one hundred." Monica paid for the three Bibles and stuffed her wallet back into her pocket. Xun Man cleared his throat but said nothing.

"So sorry." Pastor Meng smiled apologetically. "Bibles are very hard to find." He glanced at Mr. Xun again. But I will try to have more Friday. You can come back then?"

"Yes, of course. We'll see you Friday." On the way back to the bus stop, Michael whispered, "Did you see the handcuffs hooked to Xun Man's belt loop? Maybe he was going to arrest Pastor Meng if he had too many Bibles."

On the bus trip home, they prayed for Pastor Meng's safety, and that he could find more Bibles.

On Friday, Xun Man was nowhere in sight when Monica, Erika and Michael arrived at the church. Pastor Meng handed the trio a box of 100 Bibles. "I happened to have these in a back room because I have been buying them wherever I could for at least a year. But Mr. Xun does not know."

"Oh, thank you, Pastor Meng. You've done us a huge favor," Monica said as her fingers stroked the cover of the Bible she lifted out of the box.

"It's a secret," Pastor Meng said with a smile. "I like to give them to my church members. Tell the people, 'If you are asked where you got them, say you bought them.'" He grinned as if they were conspiring together.

"Thank you, thank you, thank you!" Monica's eyes sparkled as she counted out the money. Michael picked up the big box of blue-covered Bibles. "These are our favorites because they have English in one column and Chinese in the other."

On the way to the bus stop, he whispered, "Pastor Meng risked going to jail to get them for us."

"And being beaten and persecuted," Erika whispered.

"We'll tell everyone the Bibles are a gift from Jesus," Monica said. She and Erika slapped hands in a high five.

"I can't give you a high five because I'm carrying this box," Michael said.

"We know," Monica and Erika said together, grinned and slapped another high five.

The next day the team handed out Bibles to

the new believers, morning, afternoon and evening.

"You'd think we were handing out 100-dollar bills." Michael wiped his hot face on his shirttail.

Erika gazed out the classroom window at the gray fog covering the sun, and wondered what was happening in Seneca.

* * *

Thirty-five people gathered on the same corner for church the next Sunday, laughing and talking in the early morning sunshine.

"Look, there's Mr. Xun again." Monica waved and held out her hand. "I am very glad to see you this morning."

Xun Man shook her hand, but he did not smile. "You will not take these people to church," he said. "You will not take these people to church," he repeated. "Do you understand? No church today."

Monica released his hand, but her smile remained bright and warm. "Thank you for telling me." She placed her pointer finger on her chin and seemed to be thinking about something. Then her smile widened and her eyes sparkled. "We will go to the park instead."

Word spread through the crowd of children and adults: "Mr. Xun said we cannot go to the government church today. We are going to the park with Monica."

"I am sorry. I liked the dinner they served," an old lady said, leaning on her cane.

"What will we do at the park?" Joab asked. Erika couldn't help noticing his worn-out sandals.

They looked so ragged she wondered if he would walk right out of them on the way.

She hugged Abraham and his parents.

"We will have church." Monica led the way. "God doesn't care if we worship him in church or out-of-doors." She walked along the sidewalk to the park.

On the way, she motioned for Michael to walk with her. "Michael, I would like to have you speak for a few minutes on Psalm 91," she said. "Will you ask Daniel to share *Step Up To Life* with the group?" We'll sing and worship first and have your teaching and then Daniel can end our service."

Michael turned to find Daniel and Erika watched Steven move alongside Monica. "I'm glad you didn't send us home just because we couldn't go to church," he said.

"The police must think we're doing something against the government," Monica said. "They were listening to our classes more than usual yesterday."

"At least none of the Chinese have been arrested and you have not been sent back to the U.S.," Steven said.

Monica smiled at Steven and waved to a toddler along the way, but the child screamed and reached for her mother. "She hasn't seen blonde hair and blue eyes." The kind lady smiled lovingly at the little girl and her mother. The child stopped crying and gazed into Monica's eyes. Then she began to smile.

"I think she's captured by your love," Erika said from behind Monica. "I recognized your love the first time I met you too."

"And I still love you," Monica said, reaching for Erika's hand and pulling her next to her on the sidewalk.

"Erika, do you want to walk with us? I know the way," Carol asked

"Yes," Erika said. The girls linked arms and slow-jogged ahead of the group.

* * *

After the service, Monica hugged as many as she could when they left the park. She hummed the words of "Amazing Grace" to herself as she handed Erika her Bible and songbook, ready to return to the Guesthouse for lunch.

"Thank you for your help, Daniel," Monica said, falling into step next to him and Cheryl.

"I'm sure you'll have several people knocking on your door this afternoon," Cheryl said and settled her hat on her head.

"I hope so," Monica said and noticed Steven sitting on a bench nearby. "Steven, are you going to lunch?"

"Miss Wen Jing, I need to talk to you." Steven twisted his fingers in his belt loops and rose to hug her.

"Talk away," Monica said. I'll just sit on your park bench, too." she waved to Erika, Carol, Marion and the Carters on their way back to the Guesthouse and asked Steven, "Have you thought more about making Jesus Lord of your life?"

"I have," Steven said. "I didn't sleep much

last night because I was thinking so much about it. I've been looking for these answers since I was a little boy. It's taken awhile for me to make the decision but I wanted to be sure you spoke the truth before I accepted what you were saying."

"And now you're ready to talk about it?" Monica pulled SUTL out of her pocket and held it for Steven to read along with her.

"Yes, I'm ready for more information. Steven shifted on the park bench. He reached for the booklet and said, "Oh, we talked about that book Friday in Cultural Lectures."

"Yes. I like to go over *Step Up To Life* with people who are considering making Jesus Lord of their lives. It explains everything and you can decide for sure whether you want to make that decision." She turned to the first page.

*   *   *

In the afternoon, Erika played computer games at Amelia's apartment. Later, back in her room, she checked on Monica's room just as someone knocked on the door. Later on, she heard water running into the bathtub and Michael's voice as he assisted with the baptism.

No one on the team looked surprised when Steven joined them for dinner later that afternoon. "We have three new baby Christians, and Steven is one of them," Monica reported.

Steven smiled peacefully as he accepted their congratulations. "It is the best decision I have made in my entire life."

— 20 —

FINISHING THE COURSE

Erika tried not to smile but a grin threatened to crack her lips. What was Billy thinking? She'd gone to Amelia's apartment Monday after Cultural Lectures to see the photo he web cammed her.

"That's not Billy!" Erika blurted. Perfect teeth showed in the wide smile. Dark brown hair curled softly around well-shaped ears, deep blue eyes and dimples. He'd posed his arms to display massive muscles. "That's John, Billy's best friend."

Erika's passion for truth forced her to continue in spite of Amelia's sad face. "Remember, I told you Billy is short and pudgy with mousy brown hair and glasses. "He's sweet and brilliant, but he doesn't look anything like this." She still didn't mention the acne.

Silence. And tears in Amelia's eyes. So many tears that the beautiful girl hiccupped.

Erika managed to control the urge to crack up while she comforted Amelia. "What's the matter?"

"Billy's emails were so funny and sensitive, I was excited to see his photo." She wiped her eyes.

"Billy sent you emails? He hasn't sent me anything but two notes." Erika felt her face grow warm. She didn't even care if it was red.

"Oh, I am sorry, I thought he wrote to you, too." Amelia's eyes darted around the room. She fidgeted with the keyboard. The monitor went dark and she turned away from the desk. "He lied to me!"

"You got that right. What could he be—Oh, I know, he didn't want you to see what he really looks like because you're so beautiful. So John sent a photo." Erika laughed until she snorted. "Those boys are such jokers. How can we get back at them?"

Amelia smiled tight, without humor in her eyes. "He lied to me! How can I—how do you say—get him back?" She licked her lips and pursed them all at once. "I know, I'll use Photoshop and make myself ugly." Revenge sparkled in a slow grin that replaced her tears.

"Then you'll tell Billy you used Photoshop to fix the one you sent before." Erika chuckled and grabbed a chair next to Amelia.

Together the girls gave Amelia acne and windblown hair that hung in her face, and a faded shirt. "What a mess!" Amelia typed a note and told Billy she had to be honest and send a true picture. "So sorry to try to fool you the first time." Both girls doubled over with hysterics as Amelia pressed the Send button.

Erika checked her watch. "I hafta go now. Let me know if ya hear anything." She left for the

Guesthouse and promised to wait for Amelia after dinner.

At the Guesthouse, Erika told Monica about their little trick on Billy and they giggled through dinner. Back in Monica's room, she said, "Remember, we go to the hospital tonight with Michael and teach English medical terms to the doctors and nurses. The rest of the team will do English Corner." She started to load her folders into the backpack.

"Oh, I forgot. I'll have to let Amelia know I won't be walking with her to English Corner." Erika made a quick call on Monica's phone as the microphone howled in her ear.

After dinner, Monica, Erika and Michael set off for the hospital. They found the room and Professor Bing and Steven inside.

"You surprised me." Monica dropped her bag on a chair. "Let's have a group hug, a 'grug.'" Five people did the grug and stepped back for individual hugs.

"I need to make sure everything is okay on your first night." Professor Bing smiled.

"I'll help with the translation." Steven looked over the curriculum folders Monica handed him.

Professor Bing introduced Luo Medjun, a cardiologist, but the team already knew him. He had made a decision for Christ the week before in English Corner. His wife Li Chun, head nurse over 300 nurses in the hospital and responsible for their training, bowed and smiled. Erika flashed back to Monica's comment that Li Chun had attended English Corner with her husband, but she hadn't decided to follow Christ yet.

"It's so good to see you," Monica said with a bow and a smile. Michael shook their hands as Erika studied the rip in her red straw bag.

Professor Bing introduced the other members of the medical staff who had come to polish their medical English.

Monica watched Professor Bing greet more staff members across the room, and whispered, "Doctor Jun made a decision for Christ in Beijing last year when he happened to be in the city and heard about us. He attended English Corner at Petroleum University and came to our hotel to make Jesus Lord of his life. His wife left him because of his Christianity, but I asked the Holy Spirit to disciple him and I've kept email contact with him. He's really grown in the Lord."

"Praise God." Michael hugged Dr. Jun and held him for a couple of seconds in an embrace. He looked into Dr. Jun's eyes as Monica would have done. Erika wished she could look into people's eyes like that.

Then Michael looked at his watch and called the class to order. "Let's pray and ask God to help the students learn and the teachers to teach," he said.

After the prayer, Professor Bing introduced Miss Wen Jing and the team. Erika passed out study papers. For ninety minutes the group discussed medical English. At 9:00 p.m., she pointed to the clock on the wall.

"I can't believe it's nine already." Monica picked up a SUTL. "Now let's listen while Michael talks about this little booklet." She handed Erika a stack of SUTLs to pass out to the class and Michael went over the message. He dismissed them at 9:30 p.m. and invited anyone interested in the message to a discussion about it with Miss Wen Jing or himself. "You're welcome to come to Miss Wen Jing's room at the Guesthouse if you'd like to learn more."

The team packed up and Erika tapped out a secret dance when Professor Bing offered them a ride to the Guesthouse.

"You really blessed us by giving us a ride," Monica said as Michael opened the door for her and Erika.

"I enjoyed the ride too. I will park the car and come upstairs. I need to talk to you." *Professor Bing has tears in his eyes.*

"We'll be glad to talk to you." Monica did a little jig right there on the street. "Oh, look! Here comes Li Chun with Luo Medjun." She hurried to greet them next to their car.

An hour later, Erika started the water in the bathtub and held towels while Monica and Michael baptized Professor Bing and Li Chun.

Dr. Luo has tears in his eyes, Erika thought.

"Let's do a grug." Monica led the way.

"Cao Yu will probably come to see you tomorrow night." Professor Bing's wet hair dripped onto Michael, Monica and Erika.

Wet grugs are fun too.

"Tell Yu to hurry. It feels wonderful." Li Chun's

wet hair dripped on everybody too as the visitors walked out the door of Monica's apartment around midnight.

"I'm too excited to sleep," Erika said. "Oh, I know, this is the time to give you my little surprise, Monica." She put her arms around her mentor and quoted Psalm 91 all the way through without stopping.

Monica cheered, "Yeah! Great! I'm so proud of you!" She did a little happy dance around the room.

"I learned a couple of verses every night, just because I love you, Monica. I knew you wanted me to memorize the whole psalm."

"Thank you for doing that for me," Monica said. "You'll be glad you have those verses in your mind as you grow up in your Christian life. After all, it's the scripture verses in our heart that help us do what God wants us to do."

"You keep telling me that. I just don't feel it." Erika clung to her friend. "Hugs feel so good. Wish I could hug Daddy and Billy tonight."

"Maybe you will want to hug your mother someday." Monica kissed her cheek. "That will happen when God gives you the love that you didn't get from your mom and helps you forgive her. Forgiveness will help you heal."

Erika said nothing because her thoughts felt so jumbled that she didn't think she'd make sense. She opened her door and pulled her laptop out of her bag. Amelia's email erased her loneliness for the moment.

Erika, guess what! Billy emailed and apologized. He and John knew we had made up the horrible picture of me and I could not be mad at them for trying to trick me. When I got the web cam going, we laughed and joked around for a while. I wish you were here L.

See you tomorrow. You're my best friend!

Amelia

Erika snapped her laptop shut. Then she opened it again and typed an email because it was too late to IM.

I wish I could have been there too. I'm glad Billy apologized, the rogue lol. I'll really miss you too when I go back to America L. I hope you decide to come to America like we talked L.You're my best friend after Billy.

She thought a moment and typed some more.

I know your parents said absolutely not when we asked if you could come to America but God can change their minds. I hope you agree.

E.

She was almost asleep when she heard a knock on Monica's door, and her dreams filled with the sound of water running into a bathtub. How many more weeks till she went home? She was too sleepy to figure it out. And besides, China could be a nice place. With the right people around.

— 21 —

COUNTDOWN TO HOME

"One week till we leave and Mr. Xun is still not a Christian." Monica paced the brick walk in front of the Buddha statue. "Lord, bring this precious man to yourself."

Erika applied lip-gloss. *My face and hands show bad damage from the hot sun and smog, but what is a girl to do?* She pulled on her ear and felt it peeling from her sunburn at the Great Wall. Maybe she could hide out at home till everything healed, or figure out a way to camouflage the defects. If only she could cover the ache in her heart from missing her father.

She couldn't wait to wear different clothes. Why had Monica said four shorts outfits would be enough for this trip? Erika had barely worn her long pants and skirt, but the others now looked faded to muddy whatever—lime green, red, blue, khaki.

Suddenly Mr. Xun appeared on the walkway in front of them.

"Hello, Mr. Xun, so glad to see you," Monica said and nodded slightly.

He nodded back. "I decided to walk to the office today."

Monica grabbed both of his hands. "When can we talk more about Jesus? He loves you so much."

"Not now. I need to go to my office." Mr. Xun studied the statue without looking at Monica. Erika wondered why he insisted on being rude.

"I'm going home in a week and I really need to talk to you." Monica checked her pocket calendar. "How about tomorrow? Can we meet for lunch?"

Mr. Xun cleared his throat and took a little side step. His hand curled around his chin and he studied the concrete walkway. "Okay, we will meet tomorrow for lunch at the Smell Café. Should I pick you up in my car?"

Erika suppressed a giggle. She knew the Chinese had trouble pronouncing the real name, *Smile*, and she thought *Smell* might be a better name after all, especially if the bathroom happened to be located close to their table.

"No, thank you. That will be a lovely walk up the hill, just past the Administration Building. Shall we meet around twelve?" Monica's eyes danced.

When is a walk at noon lovely in this heat? Erika wondered.

"Fine, I will see you around noon." Mr. Xun walked past them, on toward his office, and Monica joined Erika on the park bench. "Tomorrow at noon! I'll have to call Charlotte for prayer. And I'll ask Gloria to come interpret, just to be sure he understands everything."

"Couldn't Gloria lose her job at CU if Mr. Xun

realizes she's a Christian?" Erika checked the ends of her braid for split ends.

"Yes, but she's so in love with Jesus that she will want to interpret for us." Monica prayed out loud for Mr. Xun all the way back to the Guest-house.

* * *

The next day, Gloria, Erika, Monica and Mr. Xun gathered at a table in the Smile Café. "I've never seen so much smoke," Erika said and coughed. She watched as men puffed away on cigarettes everywhere in the restaurant. A handwritten sign had been tacked to the wall. *Does it say "smoke here a lot"?* She wondered.

Mr. Xun smiled apologetically. "Most of the men in China smoke and there are no restrictions. I apologize for the big clouds in this restaurant."

Monica didn't seem to notice the atmosphere. "Jesus loves you, you need him," she repeated for the umpteenth time since the van trip in June.

"I cannot proclaim Jesus," Mr. Xun said. "I am the head of the University and a Communist Party Secretary. I have helped arrest Christians and put them in prison."

"People who realize Jesus loves them enough to die for them will give up everything to follow him," Monica said. "Let's go over this booklet to make sure you have all the information you need to make a decision to follow Christ. You can't make a decision without knowing your options. Let's read this book again to be sure you know your options." Monica opened the booklet and they read SUTL together with Gloria interpreting.

Erika counted back to at least four times he'd heard it in the classes, but he seemed to have forgotten much of what he'd heard before.

"Will you accept Jesus as your Savior?"

Mr. Xun sat in silence for a moment. Gloria took a sip of water. Erika applied lip-gloss and Monica sat looking at this VIP in the Communist world.

"Okay, I will do what you say. I will accept Jesus. I may go to prison but I have been looking for him for a long time. Please tell me how."

The three ladies celebrated with their hands lifted in praise. Monica read through the last two pages again with Mr. Xun as the diners around them stared intensely in their direction.

"Welcome to the family of God," Monica said and grabbed his hand. "You do realize that you will need to make Jesus Lord of your life?" Mr. Xun nodded. "He will be your only God. You cannot worship any other god."

"I want to accept Jesus, regardless, " he said.

"I'm so happy for you, Mr. Xun," Erika said, shaking his hand. "I made the same decision May first and I am thankful I did."

Monica shook his hand again.

"Now to baptize you. You must be baptized." She looked around as if she expected a baptistry to come walking in the door.

"We could take him to our usual place," Erika said. If Monica didn't care who heard them, she didn't either.

Monica appeared in deep thought, then her face brightened. Suddenly she grabbed the pitcher of ice water and dumped it over Mr. Xun's head.

"Hooooh!" He jerked out of his seat and sat back down when Monica said, "I baptize you in the name of the Father, the Son and the Holy Spirit." She closed her eyes for a moment and quoted, "If the Son therefore shall set you free, you shall be free indeed."

"You surprised me." Mr. Xun grabbed a wad of napkins to blot the water off his head and clothes.

"It just seemed the thing to do." Monica's eyes twinkled as she reached into her bag for a *Jesus* video and another SUTL to replace the waterlogged one on the table.

Mr. Xun accepted the items and stood up. "I must get back to the office." He rushed out the door as Monica called out that she'd bring him a Bible.

"Thank you," he said over his shoulder and kept on walking.

"Thank you, Gloria, for interpreting." Then Monica looked deep into Erika's eyes. "And thank you, too, for coming along. I'm sure you were praying?"

"Oh, yeah!" Erika picked up the soggy napkins and tossed them into a pile. "I wouldn't have missed it for a cheeseburger and fries at McDonald's." She grinned at Gloria, who grinned back.

Monica laid a large tip on the table and smiled apologetically at the server. "I am sorry we made such a mess," she said and Gloria interpreted.

"I am happy to clean it up," the server said

with a smile.

Monica shook the young girl's hand and introduced Gloria and Erika. Everyone shook hands. "Thank you for cleaning up the mess." With another apologetic smile and a bow, she handed the server a SUTL and led the way out the door. "We have to give Mr. Xun a Bible," she said.

The next day Monica and Erika carried one into Mr. Xun's office. "I'm bringing this to Mr. Xun." Monica smiled into the assistant's eyes.

He looked shocked. "You are delivering this to the party secretary?" Erika chuckled behind her hand.

"Yes, he wants it."

"What?" The man fumbled with the Bible and almost dropped it.

"I told him yesterday I'd bring him a Bible."

The assistant sighed and placed it in a box by a door with shiny gold characters. *That's probably Mr. Xun's name on that door*, she thought. Monica said "hello" and nodded to everyone as she walked out of the office, handing everyone a SUTL.

Tomorrow they would tell their students goodbye and pack for home. Erika sighed. She'd miss China after all, she realized. Not the smog and the heat, but the people. How could anyone help loving these dear people? Especially Amelia and the other Chinese teens. *Michael is easy to love, too*, she thought. *And Jesse.*

— 22 —

FORBIDDEN CITY

August 20, 2006, 4:00 a.m. in Beijing

Erika did the happy dance around their hotel room. "I'm going home! Home! Home! Tomorrow!" Then she stopped, yawned and took another slow turn around the room. "But I'll really miss Amelia. And Michael. And Jesse too."

Monica stretched and yawned. "You'll see Michael and Jesse at church."

"But not every day like here."

"Maybe we can have an after-China party and invite them." Monica checked Martin's papers as if she feared losing them and slipped them back into her carry-on bag.

"Good idea! And Billy could come too. And Michael could have one later, and Jesse too."

Monica playfully swatted her friend's back and sang, "The bus will pick us up at five."

"I'll be ready," Erika sang back. She hummed in the shower and dressed in her washed-out lime green outfit. Back in the room, she whined, "I could just trash these faded clothes right now." She slung her grayed-out sleep shirt onto her bed, and yawned.

"Come on, it's time to catch the bus," Monica said and yawned too.

Erika checked the mirror. "I'm really gonna miss the rest of the team like crazy bad." Daniel, Cheryl and Jesse planned to visit old friends in Chengdu for a week. Robert and Michael joined a tour group seeing the Great Wall and other tourist spots. They all planned to fly home next week, but Monica had to leave earlier than the others and get back to her job as a nurse.

Erika felt a pang of loneliness for Amelia, her smart and funny friend. What was she doing this morning? How many times had Billy emailed her since Erika left Nanchong? She glanced lovingly at the beautiful pink straw bag Amelia had given her. She flashed back to their farewell dinner in her parents' apartment.

"I just love this bag," she said. "I'll keep it forever to remember Amelia. She said she'd keep the pillow with 'Seneca, Kansas' on it too, to remember me."

Erika sighed and held up her lip-gloss. "Look, I have just barely enough to make it home."

"You've grown up a lot this summer, and I notice you aren't using as much of that stuff." Monica wrapped her arms around Erika's shoulders and then released her.

"Remember how I applied it like every few minutes all the way from Seneca to Nanchong that first day? I was like so nervous." Erika pulled her ponytail through the hole in her lime green ball cap that used to match her shorts and top.

"Yes, I know, but everything worked out, didn't it?"

"Uh huh, I really miss Amelia this morning."

"I miss everyone too, and we'll plan to come back next year. In the meantime there are emails."

"And instant messages."

Monica changed the subject. "And you're beginning to think more about Jesus and others than yourself. I'm really proud of you." She placed her straw hat on her head. "Let's go."

Five minutes later, Erika adjusted her cap and glanced down at her scuffed sandals as she waited for the shiny new tour bus door to open. "Uh! Blenk! I'm not gonna miss this part with all the dust and diesel fuel." She and Monica stepped onto the bus along with thirty other English as a Second Language China volunteers. This tour was ESLGC's final thank you before they left for America the next morning.

"Well, hello, Mr. Tom." Monica reached out to shake the tour guide's hand. "Do you remember Erika and me from the Great Wall tour?"

"Yes!" He shook their hands and smiled so big his gold molar flashed. "Welcome aboard, ladies."

"Thank you, and God bless you. He loves you, you know." Monica smiled at a little old lady who pushed past them. Mr. Tom didn't answer.

"It feels like a holiday mood." Monica and Erika mingled with the other ESLGC volunteers, talking and exchanging contact information on their last outing together.

Half an hour later, Monica gave a little bounce on the vinyl bus seat. "Here we are. In all my trips to China, I've never toured the Forbidden City." She pointed and said, "or Tiananmen Square or Chairman Mao Tsung's tomb over that way. I wish we'd asked Mr. Tom to take us there too.

"Yeah, sorta." Erika stretched her neck, trying to catch a glimpse of Tiananmen Square.

The pair walked a few steps toward the City and a Chinese family surrounded them. "Blonde hair, blue eyes. Take your picture?"

How did Erika know Monica would say yes? She crossed her arms and waited in the shade of a tree as she watched families and individuals line up to have their picture taken with Monica. Some noticed Erika's auburn hair and nutmeg eyes and asked her to join them, but she shook her head no. One little girl inspected her freckles and asked something in Chinese, but Erika didn't understand. *I feel like a freak in a circus show,* she thought to herself.

She flashed back to Mr. Tom's lecture: "Emperors from the Ming Dynasty built the Forbidden City. They believed it was the center of the world, and the sacred seat of power." He said the rooms in the complex were arranged as boxes within boxes, making them so dark that candles burned at all times.

Erika smelled the live chickens before she saw them and guessed the merchant carrying them would sell them at the open market she'd seen outside the gate. Two women, probably his wife and daughter, lugged baskets of melons behind him. A female tourist's perfume soothed her senses in the steamy air.

Two hours passed and everyone with a camera finally left. "Let's check with... ." Monica pointed to a spot just inside the gate. "Our tour bus was sitting right there and now it's gone."

"It must have left while I used the restroom." Erika stopped applying sunscreen and stared open-mouthed. "I don't see anyone from our group... . Are we lost?"

"Could be, but Jesus knows where we are and he has a plan." Monica tipped her water bottle for a drink. "Only an inch left." Erika checked the backpack and found one more bottle but it felt warm from the sun.

"We'll drink it anyway," Monica said. "At least it's wet and it will help our dry throats."

"I was really looking forward to a tour. Michael said there are no idols in the Forbidden City Temple of Heaven and I wanted to see it." Erika poured half the bottle into Monica's.

"Yes, because some believe the emperor had become a Christian and worshipped the one true God." Monica sipped her water.

"Our group musta left when you were posing for all those pics," Erika said.

"That was fun." Monica's eyes twinkled for a moment and then she got really serious. "I'm sorry we missed the tour because I know how much you were looking forward to it."

"That's okay," Erika said and pasted on a smile. She sighed and sipped water from her bottle. Silence hung between the two friends for a moment until Erika said, "So where do we go from here?"

"Let's see... . Monica stared past the gate and mumbled something to herself. She led Erika out the front gate of the Forbidden City, past the guards, across the moat and into the Imperial City, where the ancient emperors had built government offices, parks and shops.

Erika flashed back to Mr. Tom's lecture. "The city of Beijing sprawls just past the Imperial City, and open fields and rural areas lie beyond."

"I wonder if anyone speaks English." Monica tried. "Do you speak English? Hot day today." Everyone smiled and kept on walking.

"There's a motorized rickshaw. We can ride it back to—what hotel? I didn't check the name when we flew in from Nanchong at two this morning, and I was barely awake when we left again at five."

"Me too." Erika shared a few crackers she found in the backpack. "Oooh, my nose stings," she said, "and no wonder. Look at the rickshaw that man has, loaded with—what? Huge bags of reeking garbage tied with string?"

"Yes," Monica said but Erika could tell she was thinking about something else. She checked her purse. "Plenty of American money here, but only one Yuan. I had everything exchanged for the trip back to America."

The hot sidewalk seared through Erika's sandals as they wandered near the gate and the guards.

"Ah, there's a rickshaw driver without a load." Monica rushed into the street and Erika followed. "I have one Yuan, will you take us to the hotel?" She didn't tell him she had no idea of the hotel's name. Erika stepped back for a bicycle to pass.

"Ha, ha, ha." At least he laughed the same as Americans. "You need ten Yuan." Erika could barely understand his English.

"Will you take American dollars?" Monica waved one from her purse.

"No."

"That came out clear enough." Erika stepped back onto the sidewalk, away from the street crowded with cars and buses loading and unloading tourists, and Monica followed her back into the Forbidden City.

"Mr. Tom said that in ancient times only the royal families could enter the City, with its bright yellow tile roofs on every building. Intruders were killed."

"Good. You remembered." Monica smiled and patted Erika's arm. "Lord, we're here for a reason," she prayed. "We'll stay right here until you give us further directions."

They walked closer to the gate. A guard turned and made eye contact with Monica. She smiled. "They know we're here." Monica prayed, "Lord, I claim this man for Jesus," as a hunched□over man hobbled past. "I claim every man, woman and child walking through this gate." On and on she prayed, lifting up individual tourists in the throngs moving into Forbidden City. Diesel fumes and dust hovered in the 100-degree air.

Monica looked at her watch, set on American Central time for the trip home. "I'm not thirsty or hungry, are you?"

"Not really, come to think of it."

"Thank you, Jesus, for taking such good care of us." Monica smiled at four schoolgirls walking by. "Hello, I'm Monica Moore from America and this is Erika Slade."

One of the girls smiled and stepped forward a little. "Hello. We like your hair, and your eyes are, how do you say, blue?"

Lord, they speak English, Erika rejoiced silently.

"Yes," Monica said and ran her fingers through her short hair.

The girls looked at Erika. "And yours is red?"

"Auburn."

"With brown eyes? But not as brown as ours?"

"Uh, yes." Erika twizzled her braid and waited for the usual comment about her freckles, but it didn't come. Then she noticed one of the girls sported large brown freckles sprinkled across her nose. Another girl wore her hair in a thick braid down her back, the same as Erika.

"You speak excellent English. I haven't found anyone who speaks enough that I can understand." Monica quickly explained their situation.

"We will interpret for you," one of the girls said and introduced herself as Chike.

"Oh, thank you! We prayed that Jesus would send an interpreter. Please explain to the guards at the gate why we've been here so long. They've been watching us."

"Okay." The group walked to the gate where the girls explained the situation. The guards smiled and rocked back on their heels.

"We feel sorry for the leader of the English as a Second Language group who lost you," the younger guard said, and Chike interpreted for the Americans.

"Thank you for helping us." Monica and Erika gave each girl a hug.

Erika inspected the manicure she'd given herself for the trip home while Monica handed each girl a SUTL in her choice of English or Mandarin."

"Thank you," each girl said as they exchanged puzzled looks.

"Read this little book and it will tell you about Jesus."

"We have to go home now before our parents worry," Chike said. "Goodbye, and we hope you find your group." They waved and walked on, discussing the SUTLs between them.

The girls glanced through the little booklets as they turned toward home.

"Lord, help those dear girls to know you," Monica prayed and Erika said, "Amen." They wandered through the crowds with Monica praying quietly to herself, "Lord, you know where we are… . I've prayed for all these people… . It's been four hours… ."

"Plus two hours taking pictures," Erika said, but Monica must have been so focused upon her prayers that she didn't answer.

Sometime around four, the pair crossed the moat into the Imperial City and entered what looked like a hardware store. "We don't know where our hotel is." Monica explained their situation to the only clerk who could understand English. "We're Christians and we know Jesus will take care of us."

Erika thought she agreed, but she wasn't sure. *I hope I'm more like Monica some day,* she thought.

The clerk said, "I've heard about that," and Erika couldn't stop a big grin. She recognized the Chinese code words acknowledging one was a Christian. She knew they should not say anything to draw attention to this secret believer because he could be persecuted if the officials knew he was a Christian. He looked thoughtful and seemed to ask the manager in Chinese for advice.

"Call the Beijing Hotel," the manager said, and the clerk interpreted. "I will call for you," he said.

"Oh, thank you so much. I really appreciate your help." Monica tossed her empty water bottle into the trash.

The clerk called the hotel and gave them the information about Monica and Erika. "Is this the hotel?" he asked in English, probably as a courtesy to the Americans. "They don't know the name of their hotel." Slowly he replaced the receiver. "They won't tell me."

Monica smiled and said nothing. *I know Chinese policy is to be secretive*, Erika thought. They looked around at the crowd gathering around them. The clerk told the onlookers about the situation in Chinese.

"Call the American Embassy," a little freckled man spoke in English from the back of the group. "I'm sure you've been reported lost. The Embassy closes at five." It was 4:45 p.m.

"Thank you," Monica said and chuckled.

She firmly believes nothing happens by accident, Erika thought. She couldn't wait to tell Billy about this experience—in person.

The clerk dialed the number and handed the receiver to Monica. She gave them her information, listened and hung up. "Your name is Monica Moore," she quoted "Do you know that? You are with the English as a Second Language China Group. You are reported lost. Okay. Your hotel is called Beautiful Lady Hotel, and you are to get back there right now because they are frantic about you." The clerk interpreted for the Chinese around them, and they all laughed.

He called for a taxi and explained to the driver in Chinese that Monica had only American money. "Will you take them back to the Beautiful Lady Hotel?"

"Yes, I'd be glad to," the driver replied in English.

"Thank you for your help," Monica said to the clerk.

"I'm glad to help another Christian," he whispered and Monica and Erika gave him a grug.

The two friends settled against the seat in the

taxi. "We knew everything would be okay because we're Christians and Jesus always takes care of us," Monica said.

They pulled away from the hardware store, and the driver shoved a tape into the player. Music filled the taxi.

"That's Christian music! You're a Christian!" Monica and Erika clapped and sang along to the words of "Nothing But The Blood of Jesus."

"Yes, I've heard of that," the driver said, and told them about the house church he attended.

"Here is the Beautiful Lady Hotel," he said. "I hope you enjoy your trip back to America."

Monica paid the fare and said, "May I give you a hug? I'm a grandma and I give grandma hugs."

"Yes," he said and hugged her right there on the street.

Erika crossed her arms and waited by the taxi.

It had been more than five hours since the Americans realized they were alone by the Forbidden City gate.

* * *

Monica chuckled as she walked up to Mr. Tom and Mr. Jao, the Communist officer and Chinese representative for the group, pacing up and down the lobby.

Mr. Jao stopped mid-pace and jabbed a finger in the air. "We lost these ladies, this blonde and this redhead."

"We're not lost, we're okay." Monica chuckled.

"Ahhh!" Mr. Jao sounded frustrated and angry.

For the rest of the evening, Monica was not known by her name, but as the lady who was lost.

"If you're lost in Beijing," Monica told her group members, "or anywhere else, just ask the Lord to find Christians and they will get you back to where you need to be."

— 23 —

HOME

"I'll watch till China disappears." Erika's nose almost touched the window as the Air China jet headed east over the Pacific toward Chicago.

Monica dabbed her eyes.

Erika wrapped her mentor's shoulders in a hug and gave a little seat-leap. "Uh, sorry to be totally rude today, but I'm soooo glad to be going home." She adjusted her pillow and ran her fingers over her beautiful pink bag. "Fourteen-hour countdown. I can't wait. But I will miss Amelia and Carol. And Marion. And Elizabeth. Oh, and helping with the classes. That was a lot of fun."

Monica sighed and leaned back in her seat. "I must pray for China." Erika knew her friend's mind list because she had heard it often over the past two months.

She napped and dreamed of hamburgers loaded with the works and a double hot fudge sundae on top of chewy brownies in a huge blue bowl, similar to the ones she and Billy shared at the Busy Burger Drive-In back home. She awoke with a start when the flight attendant set a tray with French fries and Coke in front of her. Salivating and cheering, she said, "Gimme a cheeseburger and it can't get any better than this."

She eyed the peanuts on her seatmates' trays. "Are you going to eat those?" she asked, pointing.

"No, help yourself." The man sitting on the other side of Monica handed his to Monica and she dropped both bags onto Erika's tray.

"A hot dog it's not," Erika said around the food in her mouth, "but at least it's not rice, or snake, or eyeballs."

She finished everything on her tray and grabbed her bag. "Where's the restroom? Oh yeah, I see the sign. Excuse me," she said as she stepped over both seatmates' feet.

The bathroom smelled so sweet. No eye-watering stench like she'd endured for two months. Well, a little maybe, but not overpowering.

Fifteen minutes later she scrambled over her seatmates' feet again and settled against the window. Then she yawned and went back to sleep.

"Jesus is your best friend... ." Monica's statement woke Erika.

"What time is it?" she yawned.

"It's four p.m., Dear. Meet Al. He just accepted Christ."

Erika reached in front of Monica to shake his hand. "Isn't Monica just a wonder? I sleep and she's busy talking about Jesus." She yawned again.

Erika wished she could share Jesus like Monica

did. She applied lip-gloss and pounded the last traces of nail polish out of the bottle for a touch-up."

Erika squirmed and looked out the window. *I still need to forgive Daddy's killers and Mom*.

Monica kept talking to Al.

Just a few hours and she'd see Mom again. Erika bounded out of her seat and headed for the restroom. She needed a moment alone to stop the feelings of desperation that started to close in.

Al had moved across the aisle to talk to someone when Erika returned to her seat. She plopped down and turned to search her dear friend's eyes.

"I wanna get ridda that bird blob on my nose." The feelings inside threatened to cut off her breathing.

"What? Oh." Compassion filled Monica's eyes and Erika read genuine love in their depths. "I understand."

Monica reached for her hand. "I'm glad you realize that in order to move on in life, we must forgive, regardless. Your father's killers won't apologize and your mother doesn't seem to recognize what she's doing. You may never forget the bad things that happened, but since you want to forgive the people who did these things, God will help you and give you peace."

"Think I should pray." Erika put her other hand over Monica's and bowed her head. "Father," she began, "I want to forgive Daddy's killers and Mom. Please help me." She sat quietly, eyes closed as everything around her faded away and she felt

Jesus close enough to touch.

His smile filled the area around their seats and her heart slowly morphed into golden peace. She nestled in Jesus' love. Monica seemed far away, still holding Erika's hand.

"I've never felt peace like this," Erika whispered. Monica's hand tightened on hers. Al snapped his laptop case shut. People walked up and down the aisle. A baby cried.

"Would you like something to drink?" The flight attendant's voice grated harsh on Erika's heart, but she focused on the kind face framed with curly brown hair.

"Yes, please. I'll have a Coke." She reached for the soda and the peace didn't dissolve as she was afraid it would. It stayed with her all the way home. Maybe she'd have it forever.

*　　*　　*

Fourteen hours after takeoff in China, Erika kissed the ground in Seneca, Kansas, and Monica chuckled. The airport lacked an enclosed walkway and they headed across the asphalt for the terminal. "Just like China," the weary teen whined. She opened her mouth to speak again and the wind blew dust into it. Her jaws snapped shut and her teeth gritted, the same way they did in China. The stench of rotting garbage from a nearby dumpster stung her nose. Another passenger passed them with a St. Bernard puppy. Out of nowhere the clouds opened and dumped a downpour.

"Eeek! I feel like I'm still in China," Erika said,

ducking under Monica's umbrella. "Watch out, here comes the family."

Ignoring the rain, Billy and John nearly bowled the travelers over with bear hugs and cheers. Mom gave Monica a huge hug under the umbrella, then turned her back on Erika.

What do I do now? Erika wondered. "Hi, Mom," she squeaked. *Mom won't look at me... . I'll hug her anyway.* Throwing her arms across Mom's back, she said firmly, "Hi, Mom."

Billy, John and Monica laughed and clapped as they formed a semi-circle around mother and daughter.

Mom glanced at the group. Slowly, hesitantly, she turned and reached out to Erika for a half-hug. "Welcome home," she mumbled.

She didn't say she missed me, though. Maybe it's a start.

"Let's go get the luggage." Monica linked arms with Mom and they led the way.

Billy and John fell into step next to Erika. "You hugged Mom, I'm proud," Billy mumbled so Mom wouldn't hear. "I'm doing more of that too." And I'm talking to her a lot about coming to church with us, like Monica said." The threesome marched in step through the airport doors to the luggage carousal, laughing and celebrating.

Erika felt her thoughts of China fade into the misty area between fantasy and reality. *I will think about China later,* she thought. *Right now I need to hug Monica*.

Monica returned the hug, warm and cozy as

always. They laughed together and Erika whispered, "Thank you for China in my life."

APPENDIX A

Monica and Steven look at *Step Up To Life*

Continued from Chapter 19, page 191

"Miss Wen Jing, I need to talk to you." Steven twisted his fingers in his belt loops and rose to bow to her.

Monica returned the bow. "Talk away. I'll just sit on your park bench, too." She waved to Erika, Carol, Marion and the Carters on their way back to the Guesthouse and asked Steven, "Have you thought more about making Jesus Lord of your life?"

"I have," Steven said. "I didn't sleep much last night because I was thinking so much about it. I've been looking for these answers since I was a little boy. It's taken awhile for me to make the decision but I wanted to be sure you spoke the truth before I accepted what you were saying."

"And now you're ready to talk about it?" Monica pulled SUTL out of her pocket and held it for Steven to read along with her.

"Yes, I need more information." Steven shifted on the park bench. He reached for the booklet and said, "Oh, we talked about that book Friday in Cultural Lectures."

"Yes. I like to go over *Step Up To Life* with people who are considering making Jesus Lord of their lives. It explains everything and you can decide for sure whether you want to make that decision." She turned to page one.

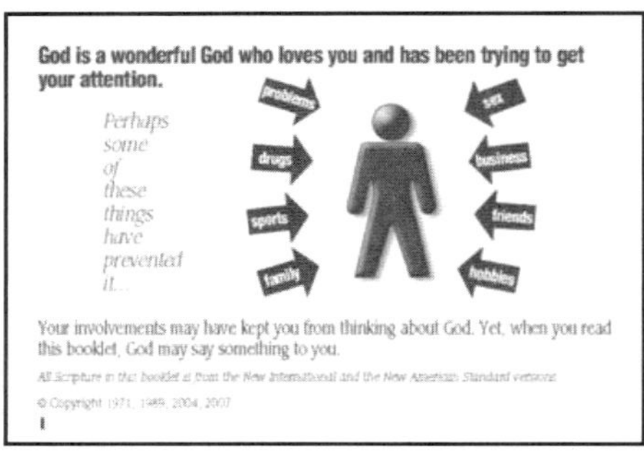

God is a wonderful God who loves you and has been trying to get your attention.

Perhaps some of these things have prevented it…

problems
drugs
sports
family
sex
business
friends
hobbies

Your involvements may have kept you from thinking about God. Yet, when you read this booklet, God may say something to you.

All Scripture in this booklet is from the New International and the New American Standard versions.

© Copyright 1971, 1989, 2004, 2007

1

"God is a wonderful God who loves you and has been trying to get your attention," she read, pointing to the human figure in the graphic.

"Perhaps some of these things have prevented it… . Problems… . friends… . business… . family. Have you found that many things keep you from thinking about God?"

Steven's eyes darted around the playground as he watched the children climbing on the play equipment. "Yes. But I thought about him a lot last night."

"You already know something about God from Cultural Lectures and English Corner, but here are three important truths you should consider now." Monica pointed to the top of page two.

"God is all wise and knows what is best for your life." She paused and then read the second and third points:

2) "He is holy, cannot approve of sin and will judge it. And—

3) He is merciful so He can hold back judgment and pardon you because of Christ's death on the cross."

She finished reading that section: "Jesus Christ is the only way to God, for he said "...I *am the way and the truth and the life. No one comes to the Father except through me*." John 14:6.

"What is the highest purpose for living, Steven?" Monica looked at him rather than the book because she'd memorized that part. "Could it be your family, to be happy, to live a good life? To be fulfilled?" She quoted John 17:3, *"Now this is eternal life, that they may know you, the only true God, and Jesus Christ, whom you have sent*." She waited for his answer.

He squinted at the sunlight filtering through the trees. "My highest purpose has always been to do outstanding work at school and please the Communist officials." Steven glanced at the next page as Monica turned to it.

"This wonderful God wants to forgive your sins, give you meaning in your life now, and take you to heaven when you die," she read. "All this is yours, Steven, when you submit to the Lord Jesus Christ." She pointed to the next line, "Therefore, the most important question you will ever face is—'Who runs your life? You or Jesus?'"

Steven studied his fingernails without responding.

"The next few pages will help you find out," Monica assured him.

He glanced curiously at page four and the graphic with stair-steps. "What—?"

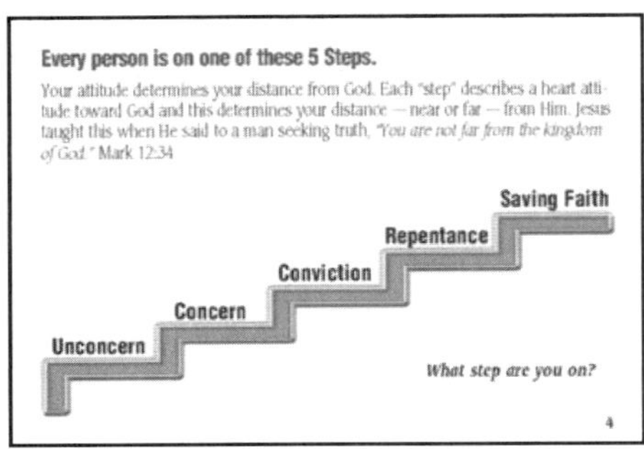

"Every person is on one of these five steps," Monica declared, looking into Steven's eyes, not at the page. "Unconcern, Concern, Conviction, Repentance, or Saving Faith... . Which step are you on?"

Steven squirmed. "I'm not sure. Before Friday night I didn't think a lot about it, but since we read that page on Conviction, I ... I think I'm on the next-to-the-last step, Repentance."

"Yes, I agree." Monica skipped to page nine with 'Repentance' in big letters at the top. Then she let the pages fan through her hands and said, "But let's look at pages seven and eight first, 'Conviction.' Remember, we read these pages with the class Friday evening in English Corner?"

"Yes," Steven said, "and I've been thinking about those stair-steps ever since."

"Do you hope to go to heaven by 'being good' or 'doing the best you can?'" She read aloud and Steven followed along. "The questions you must ask yourself are, 'Am I good enough? Have I kept God's commandments —100 percent— in thought, word and deed? If you have, then you can go to heaven by your good life. *However, through the law we become conscious of sin*. Romans 3:20."

"I think that's what I did," Steven said. "After Friday night I became conscious of my sin and how I need to ask Jesus to help me."

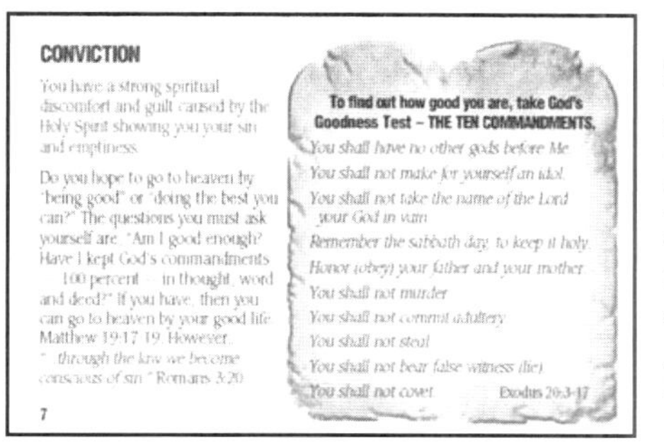

CONVICTION

You have a strong spiritual discomfort and guilt caused by the Holy Spirit showing you your sin and emptiness.

Do you hope to go to heaven by "being good" or "doing the best you can?" The questions you must ask yourself are: "Am I good enough? Have I kept God's commandments — 100 percent — in thought, word and deed?" If you have, then you can go to heaven by your good life. Matthew 19:17-19. However, "...through the law we become conscious of sin." Romans 3:20

7

To find out how good you are, take God's Goodness Test – THE TEN COMMANDMENTS.

You shall have no other gods before Me.
You shall not make for yourself an idol.
You shall not take the name of the Lord your God in vain.
Remember the sabbath day, to keep it holy.
Honor (obey) your father and your mother.
You shall not murder.
You shall not commit adultery.
You shall not steal.
You shall not bear false witness (lie).
You shall not covet. Exodus 20:3-17

Monica pointed to a box on page seven: "To find out how good you are, I'll help you take God's Goodness Test, THE TEN COMMANDMENTS."

"I took the test after I got home Friday evening, and I didn't do so well." Steven grinned sheepishly and pulled his own SUTL from his pocket.

"Steven, it looks like you've been reading and rereading that SUTL since Friday evening," she said. "I see you've made notes all over it and it shows a lot of wear."

"I think your God has a hold on me and He won't let go," Steven said.

"Let's look at the Ten Commandments again," Monica said. "Remember, Jesus said that if you break even one commandment, you're guilty and cannot get into heaven by yourself. You need Jesus' help."

Steven found the Commandments in his book and read, *YOU SHALL HAVE NO OTHER GODS BEFORE ME*.

Monica waited a moment to allow him to comment.

"That means, don't have anything you like to do more than worship God, read his word the Bible and give him glory," Steven said.

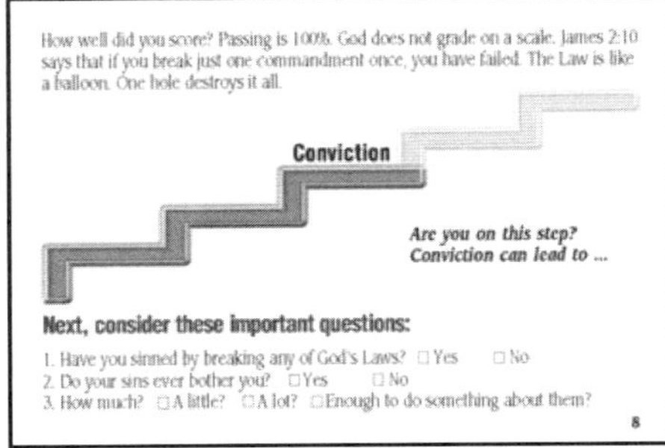

How well did you score? Passing is 100%. God does not grade on a scale. James 2:10 says that if you break just one commandment once, you have failed. The Law is like a balloon. One hole destroys it all.

Conviction

Are you on this step?
Conviction can lead to ...

Next, consider these important questions:

1. Have you sinned by breaking any of God's Laws? ☐ Yes ☐ No
2. Do your sins ever bother you? ☐ Yes ☐ No
3. How much? ☐ A little? ☐ A lot? ☐ Enough to do something about them?

8

Monica smiled. *This brilliant man could probably quote all of the Ten Commandments by heart,* she thought. "You are correct, Steven. God doesn't want us to love anything more than we love him. Not family, not job, not money or anything else." She paused and watched a bug crawling across the end of the park bench next to her. "I know I've loved many things more than I love God. I've broken this first commandment."

YOU SHALL NOT MAKE FOR YOURSELF AN IDOL, Steven read. "Gold and silver idols are an insult to God because he's so much bigger than anything humans could make."

"You're right, Steven. We cannot make anything to please God enough that he will want us to worship it." Monica watched the bug disappear over the edge of the park bench.

YOU SHALL NOT TAKE THE NAME OF THE LORD YOUR GOD IN VAIN. "I used God's name in vain many times before I became a Christian," Monica said. "I'm guilty of breaking this commandment."

Steven nodded. "Me too."

REMEMBER THE SABBATH DAY TO MAKE IT HOLY. Monica read the fourth Commandment aloud and said, "I've broken this one a lot. I've used my time on Sunday for many things besides worshipping God, being with my family and resting."

"I certainly broke it a lot because I didn't know

it existed," Steven said with a sigh.

HONOR (OBEY) YOUR FATHER AND YOUR MOTHER. Monica sipped water from her bottle. "I didn't always honor my parents, especially when I was little. I did better in later years, but I have many regrets."

"We honor our parents in China, but I didn't always do it with a smiling heart," Steven said. "Sometimes I complained a lot to other people before I did what my parents told me to do."

YOU SHALL NOT MURDER. Steven set his book down and crossed his legs. "I never killed anyone. I must not have broken this one."

"But I murdered other people by gossiping about them or wishing they were dead. One time I wished my teacher was dead because she embarrassed me in front of the class. I'm guilty." Monica screwed the cap back on her water bottle.

"I never thought of it that way," Steven said and read the next Commandment. *YOU SHALL NOT COMMIT ADULTERY*.

Monica looked thoughtful. "Jesus said we commit adultery when we look at another person and wish we could have sex with them. I'm guilty. I've done that."

"Now that you put it that way, I have too." Steven shifted on the park bench.

YOU SHALL NOT STEAL... . I don't remember stealing anything," he said and twizzled his ear.

"I've stolen," Monica said. "When I was a little girl I took a chocolate popsicle for myself and gave one to my friend when my parents said we couldn't have any."

"But you were probably a cute little thief,"

Steven said with a chuckle.

"God saw my actions as sin because he has told us not to steal, " Monica said. "No questions asked."

YOU SHALL NOT BEAR FALSE WITNESS (LIE). "I lied when I wanted to go to school and the teacher wouldn't let me," Steven confessed. "I told him my sister would stay home if I came, but I forgot to ask her first."

Monica chuckled. "Sometimes things seem funny but God still sees them as sin."

YOU SHALL NOT COVET. Steven said, "I do not remember what *covet* means."

"*Covet* means to want something somebody else has, such as their car, their house, their wife, their money or talent."

"I coveted my friend's family," Steven said. "He had a grandmother and mine had died. I coveted his grandma."

"Me too," Monica said and raised her red tennis shoes to look at the toes. "I've coveted my sisters' boyfriends and many, many things."

"I guess we're both guilty of all the Commandments, and I'm convicted," Steven said. He grinned sidewise at Monica and flipped the page. "I'm really glad I know what's on page ten." He pointed to the big word, *Repentance*.

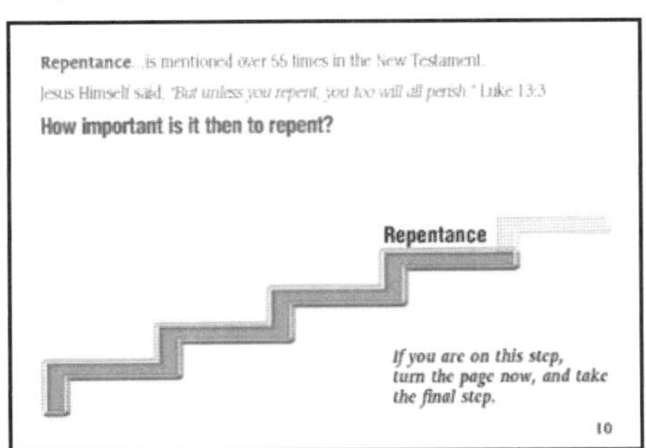

"You're right," Monica said and smiled. "When you repent you have a change of mind and heart and choose to reject and forsake all known sin and the right to run your life independently of God."

Steven read, "Repentance is the act of getting off the throne of your life so that Jesus Christ may take his rightful place there. Repentance is a spiritual u-turn necessary before you believe."

"Repentance is not just being sorry for your sins. With repentance there is sorrow, but you can have sorrow without repentance. Many people are sorry for the consequences of sin, but not sin itself. '*Godly sorrow brings repentance that leads to salvation and leaves no regret, but worldly sorrow brings death*'." 2 Corinthians 7:10.

"Repentance is not just quitting a sinful act," he read. "Some people have refrained from certain sins and reformed for personal reasons (health, reputation, family, business, etc.) not because their sins displeased God." He glanced back over the page. "Wow, I didn't know repentance meant all of that."

Repentance is mentioned more than 55 times in the New Testament," Monica said, without looking at the booklet, and Steven read the words at the top of page ten. "Jesus himself said, '*But unless you repent you too will perish.*' Luke 13:3."

SAVING FAITH IN THE LORD JESUS

You are prepared to make a total commitment of all you are and all you have to the rule of the Lord Jesus Christ.

It is a change of government in your heart from self-rule to the Lord Jesus Christ. Since Christ is God, died on the cross and rose from the dead for you, He is more important than your job, family, finances, career, and even your life itself. Matthew 10:37-39, Luke 9:57-62, 1 Corinthians 15:3,4

In Luke 14:26, Jesus says that if a person would be His disciple, he must put Him first before his father and mother, his wife and children, his brothers and sisters yes, and even his own life — or he cannot be His disciple.

When you surrender and completely trust Him in this way, God will put His Spirit in you and you will be born into His family. God now becomes your loving Father and He can make any changes in your life that He wants — anywhere, anytime.

"Believe in the Lord Jesus, and you will be saved." Acts 16:31

11

"So it is important to repent." Steven flipped to page eleven and read the big words at the top of the page, "SAVING FAITH IN THE LORD JESUS."

"You are prepared to make a complete commitment of all you are and have to the total rule of the Lord Jesus

Christ," Monica read. And then, "It is a change of government in your heart from self-rule to the Lord Jesus Christ."

Since Christ is God and died and rose from the dead for you, he is more important than your job, family, finances, career, and even your life itself. Matthew 10:37-39 and Luke 9:57-62."

Steven rubbed the page between his thumb and forefinger and read, "In Luke 14:26, Jesus says that if a person would be his disciple, he must put him (God) first before his father and mother, his wife and children, his brothers and sisters—yes, and even his own life—or he cannot be his disciple." He sat very still as if he were thinking deeply and sorting these facts out in his mind.

Monica began reading, "When you surrender and completely trust in him in this way, God will put his Spirit in you and you will be born into God's family. He now becomes your loving Lord and can make any changes in your life he wants—anywhere, any time."

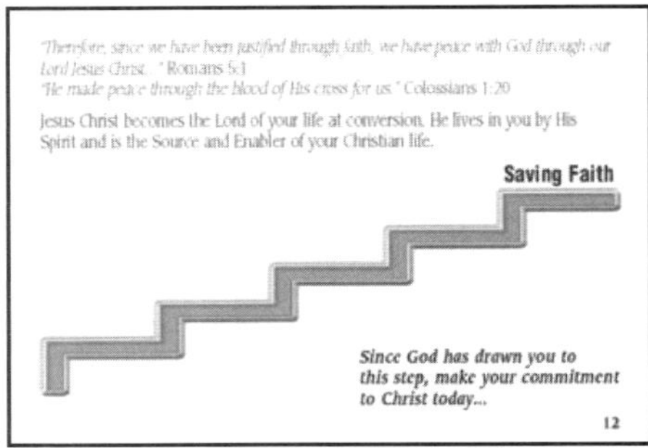

"Anywhere, any time." Steven sighed and said, "The stairway on page twelve has "Saving Faith" at the top. Is that where I'm headed?"

Monica read the small letters below the stairway: "Since God has drawn you to this step, make your commitment to Christ today..."

"But how do I do that?" Steven asked. "Oh, here it is, at the top of page-thirteen... ."

In your own words talk to God...

Confess your sins. Call them by name — pride, sexual sins, lying, unforgiveness, greed, cheating, etc.

Tell God you are repenting — willing to forsake all known sin and the root of your sins which is selfishness.

Tell God you are believing in Jesus Christ — Whom He has raised from the dead and receiving Him into your life as Lord and Savior.

He will keep His word, forgive you and come into your life, making you new.

You may make this commitment with or without deep emotions. Your reaction is determined by temperament, background and God's individual approach to you. You do know that you have committed your will to please the Lord and this is essential. Emotions will pass, but the choice of your heart remains the same.

Thank the Lord now for becoming His child and for His new life within you. YOU CAN PRAY NOW.

13

1) IN YOUR OWN WORDS TALK TO GOD—Confess your sins. Call them by name: pride, cheating, lying, immorality, greed, unforgiveness, etc."

2) TELL GOD YOU ARE REPENTING—willing to forsake all known sin and the root of your sins which is selfishness.

3) TELL GOD YOU ARE BELIEVING IN HIM—giving yourself entirely to him and receiving Jesus Christ into your life as Lord and Savior." Steven's eyes scanned the words again. "Well, that's about it, right? Will you help me, Monica? I'd like to repent now."

Together Monica and Steven bowed their heads and she led him in a prayer, using the three points they had just read. "He will keep his word, forgive you and come into your life, making you new." Monica helped Steven follow the last point on page thirteen: "THANK THE LORD NOW FOR BECOMING HIS CHILD AND FOR HIS NEW LIFE WITHIN YOU."

Steven leaned back on the bench and said, "Those last bold letters say it all. Thank you, Monica, for helping me... . I feel good right now!"

Together they rejoiced in Steven's joy and the new life he was accepting by faith. "This is the beginning of your new life, Steven, your birthday." They hugged as they rose from the park bench and started down the sidewalk toward the Guesthouse.

"It just doesn't get any better than this," Steven said and leaped into the air. "I am so happy! I have more joy than my body can hold!"

"This is the choice of your heart," Monica said, "And I rejoice with you. But your emotions will pass and some days won't feel so good. But by faith you have repented and you must write this down as your spiritual birthday. Later tonight we'll read page fourteen where it gives four reasons you can know you are saved."

Four reasons you can know you are saved:

1 You have obeyed God's commands to repent and believe, and He is faithful in keeping His Word. *"I write these things to you who believe in the name of the Son of God so that you may know that you have eternal life."* I John 5:13

2 You have confidence in the blood of Christ shed on the cross. *"In him we have redemption through his blood, the forgiveness of sins, in accordance with the riches of God's grace..."* Ephesians 1:7

3 You have renounced all claims to run your life and given Jesus Christ, the Resurrected Lord, that supreme right. *"So then, just as you received Christ Jesus as Lord, continue to live in him..."* Colossians 2:6

4 God has put His Holy Spirit right inside you – in your very spirit and gives you assurance you are His. *"The Spirit Himself bears witness with our spirit that we are children of God..."* Romans 8:16

14

"Okay," Steven said and leaped into the air again, "but right now I'm going to celebrate!"

For more information log onto: www.stepuptolife.com.

APPENDIX B

PSALM 91

1 Whoever goes to the Lord for safety, whoever remains under the protection of the Almighty, can say to Him,
2 "You are my defender and protector. You are my God; in you I trust."
3 He will keep you safe from all hidden dangers and from all deadly diseases.
4 He will cover you with his wings; you will be safe in His care; His faithfulness will protect and defend you.
5 You need not fear any dangers at night or sudden attacks during the day
6 or the plagues that strike in the dark or the evils that kill in daylight.
7 A thousand may fall dead beside you, ten thousand all around you, but you will not be harmed.
8 You will look and see how the wicked are punished.

9 You have made the Lord your defender, the
most high your protector,
10 and so no disaster will strike you, no violence
will come near your home.
11 God will put His angels in charge of you to protect you wherever you go.
12 They will hold you up with their hands to keep
you from hurting your feet on the stones.
13 You will trample down lions and snakes, fierce
lions and poisonous snakes.
14 God says, "I will save those who love Me and
will protect those who acknowledge Me as Lord.
15 When they call to Me, I will answer them; when
they are in trouble, I will be with them. I will
rescue them and honor them.
16 I will reward them with long life; I will save
them."

From: The Good News Bible

APPENDIX C

In Christ Alone I Stand

In Christ alone my hope is found,
He is my light, my strength, my song.
This cornerstone, this solid ground,
Firm through the fiercest drought and storm.
What heights of love, what depths of peace,
When fears are stilled, when strivings cease.
My comforter, my all-in-all,
Here in the love of Christ I stand.
In Christ alone who took on flesh,
Fullness of God in helpless babe,
This gift of love and righteousness.
Scorned by the ones He came to save
Til on that Cross, as Jesus died,
The wrath of God was satisfied,
For every sin on Him was laid.
Here in the death of Christ I live
There in the death of Christ I live.
Light of the world by darkness slain,
Then bursting forth in glorious days.
Up from the grave He rose again,

And as He stands in victory,
Sin's curse has lost its grip on me,
For I am His and He is mine.
Bought with the precious blood of Christ,
No guilt in life, no fear in death,
This is the power of Christ in me.
From life's first cry to final breath,
Jesus commands my destiny.
No power of hell, no scheme of man
Can ever pluck me from His hands.
Til He returns or calls me home.
Here in the power of Christ I'll stand,
Til He returns or calls me home.
Here In the power of Christ I stand,
Here in the power of Christ alone.

Written by Stuart Townsend and Keith Getty

Nothing But The Blood of Jesus

What can wash away my sin?
Nothing but the blood of Jesus.
What can make me whole again?
Nothing but the blood of Jesus.

O precious is the flow
That makes me white as snow,
No other fount I know,
Nothing but the blood of Jesus.

For my pardon this I see
Nothing but the blood of Jesus.
For my cleansing this my plea:
Nothing but the blood of Jesus.

Nothing can for sin atone:
Nothing but the blood of Jesus.
Naught of good that I have done:
Nothing but the blood of Jesus.

Writer Unknown

Jesus Loves Me

Jesus Loves me! This I know,
For the Bible tells me so.
Little ones to Him belong,
They are weak but He is strong.

Yes, Jesus loves me!
Yes, Jesus loves me!
Yes, Jesus loves me!
The Bible tells me so.

Jesus loves me! This I know,
As He loved so long ago,
Taking children on His knee,
Saying, "Let them come to me."

Jesus loves me still today,
Walking with me on my way,
Wanting as a friend to give
Light and love to all who live.

Jesus loves me! He who died
Heaven's gate to open wide,
He will wash away my sin,
Let His little child come in.

Jesus loves me! He will stay
Close beside me all the way;
Thou hast bled and died for me,
I will henceforth live for Thee.

Written by: Anna B. Warner, 1861

Audrey Hebbert, has been a freelance writer for forty years—because she had no choice—she had to write. She is a native Nebraskan, having grown up in the Sandhills. As a former columnist, teacher, and business owner, Hebbert draws material for novels, children's stories, short stories, devotionals and nonfiction articles from her broad base of experience.

Some recent sales have been to Focus on the Family's *Clubhouse*, *Highlights for Children*, *Hopscotch*, *The Quiet Hour*, *Cup of Comfort for Women*, *Cup of Comfort Devotional for Mothers*, and Standard's *Devotions*. She is a member of the Society of Children's Book Writers and Illustrators, Fellowship of Christian Writers, The Writers View2, Heartland of America Christian Writers Network, and Omaha WordSowers.

Audrey divides her time between Omaha and Kansas City, Kansas, where her two children and their families live. She loved to watch her grandson Josh race his dirt bike so much that she wrote a children's novel about him called *Dirt Bike Rider*. Publication is planned for 2008.

Visit Audrey's website at: www.audreyhebbert.com